The New York Times

CUDDLE UP WITH CROSSWORDS
75 Light and Easy Puzzles

Edited by Will Shortz

ST. MARTIN'S GRIFFIN ★ NEW YORK

ISBN-13: 978-0-312-37636-9
ISBN-10: 0-312-37636-7

First Edition: November 2007

10   9   8   7   6   5   4   3   2   1

The New York Times

CUDDLE UP WITH CROSSWORDS

ACROSS

1 "___ Marner"
6 Plopped (down)
9 Luxurious
13 To any degree
14 The Beatles' "___ Love You"
15 French income
16 Prickly plants
17 "Gotcha!"
18 Terminator
19 Train car/Strips again
21 Hooks back up/Winder
23 Chess's ___ Lopez opening
24 Early baby word
25 Time in history
28 Tennis's Sampras
30 Did a no-no/Comics pest
35 Treaty
37 Some paintings
39 Ace plus one
40 Above
41 What each word of six or more letters in this puzzle does
43 Kind of talk
44 Bo of "10"
46 60's singer Sands
47 Pencil filler
48 Writer Hubbard/Grow threefold
50 Sicilian peak
52 Blvds.
53 Profess
55 Opposite of a ques.
57 Security guard/ID at a party
61 No-goodnik/Patches, as a sweater
65 Thunderstruck
66 Without further ___

68 Tropical fruit
69 Dead duck
70 Fish off Nova Scotia
71 Vicinities
72 Squid defenses
73 US Airways competitor
74 West Yorkshire city

DOWN

1 Pouches
2 Type of type: Abbr.
3 Shoestring
4 Do tailoring on
5 Boo-boo/Students
6 Work out in a ring
7 Shade of blond
8 Pageant crown
9 Carson's successor
10 Loosen
11 Dance bit
12 For the woman
15 Newly placed/Telephoner
20 ___ newt (witch's ingredient)
22 Sullivan and Harris
24 Bring to the door/Hugely unpopular
25 Lyric poem
26 "Boléro" composer
27 Sour
29 Scrabble piece
31 Simon or Diamond
32 Art subjects
33 Brilliance

34 Scout's good works
36 Genealogy display
38 Roasting rod
42 French legislature
45 "Seinfeld" guy/Comment
49 Southern power provider: Abbr.
51 "20 Questions" category/Layer
54 Put into effect
56 Entangle
57 1958 musical
58 "Mr. X"
59 Desert Storm vehicle
60 She sheep
61 Fizzy drink
62 On bended ___
63 "Holy moly!"
64 Supreme Diana
67 ___ Jones

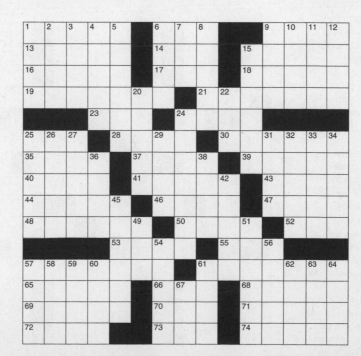

by Mary E. Brindamour

2

ACROSS

1. Artist Chagall
5. Words to live by
10. Kind of liquor
14. Coloratura's piece
15. Units to be subdivided
16. ___ vera
17. Water source
18. Financial wherewithal
19. Storm
20. Supermarket tabloid subject #1
23. Fifty-fifty
24. Hosp. procedure
25. Like marble
28. Like Charlie Chan
33. Research facility: Abbr.
34. Policy position
35. Gardner of "Show Boat"
36. Supermarket tabloid subject #2
40. Coach Parseghian
41. Exudes
42. "Stat!"
43. Romeo
45. Cars that are in the shop a lot
47. Hate grp.
48. Donaldson and others
49. Supermarket tabloid subject #3
56. Appear ahead
57. It starts with Genesis
58. Mideast carrier
60. Tulip planting
61. Sans company
62. Rhody, in an old song
63. Concerning
64. More green
65. Lockbox document

DOWN

1. Gullet
2. Geometrician's figuring
3. Brook
4. Hot, in Jalisco
5. "Out, ___ spot!": Lady Macbeth
6. Continental divide?
7. Snag
8. Darn
9. Not checking to make sure
10. 1990's Fox sitcom
11. Jai ___
12. Nike's swoosh, for one
13. Popular youth magazine
21. Woman in a garden
22. Words to live by
25. Goldsmith's "The ___ of Wakefield"
26. Start of a new año
27. Faith of five million Americans
28. Playful animal
29. Beams
30. Renaissance Italian poet
31. Birdlike
32. Reindeer herders
34. Judge, with "up"
37. Knocks on the noggin
38. Elton John or Mick Jagger
39. Three-time Masters champ
44. Like some arms
45. Soap (up)
46. Record label inits.
48. Classic 1953 western
49. Isle of exile
50. Reed and Costello
51. Electric unit
52. Seat of Allen County, Kan.
53. Sprout
54. Collagist's need
55. Sensible
59. Inc., abroad

by Hugh Davis

ACROSS

1 Regal showing
5 Arp's art
9 Kind of gun
14 Bahraini bigwig
15 Long-legged wader
16 Soft palate projection
17 Crucifix inscription
18 Grasslands
19 Quiche Lorraine ingredient
20 Like Richard I
23 Place for powder
24 Tony-winning actress Grimes
25 Do
27 Flamethrower fuel
30 Dinghy or wherry
33 "Put ___ on it!"
34 Anent
37 The end of one's rope, maybe
38 Joplin composition
39 Lloyd Webber's "___ of Love"
41 Poisonous: Prefix
42 Give a shellacking
44 Additionally
45 With 66-Across, "Romeo is Bleeding" star
46 Puffy people?
48 Kind of voyage
50 Hoopster Archibald
51 Leaf's breathing orifice
53 Cockpit abbr.
55 Like some schemes
60 Spacious
62 Humpbacked helper
63 Missile housing
64 Smart guys
65 ___-war bird (predatory flier)
66 See 45-Across

67 Not speaking to
68 Bushel and a peck
69 Undiluted

DOWN

1 Gardener's equipment
2 Former Atlanta arena
3 Joan of art
4 Pitch on paper
5 Sophie's "choice" and others
6 Perpendicular to the keel
7 Bedside book
8 Gal Fri.
9 Steam bath followers
10 She married Mickey, Artie and Frank
11 Like Chaplin's walk
12 Skin soother
13 Went off, in a way
21 Shakespearean prince
22 Author Umberto
26 Nigerian tribesman
27 They're always looking for deals
28 Burglar's bane
29 Like many a Rockwell kid
30 Enormous birds of myth
31 Together
32 Ross Perot, e.g.
35 Places to get 9-Down
36 ___ Avivian
39 February birthstone

40 Procrastinator's word
43 Dossier letters
45 Go-between
47 "Bad Behaviour" star Stephen
49 Doc bloc
51 "Love Story" author
52 Butchery selection
53 Composer Khachaturian
54 "Whatever ___ Wants" (1955 song)
56 What swish shots miss
57 Shade of green
58 Lamb's pen name
59 Word of warning
61 Former name of Universal Studios

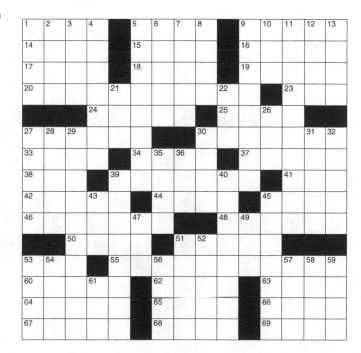

by Mark Elliot Skolsky

4

ACROSS

1 More than dislike
6 Big name in computer games
10 Fish from Dover
14 Be loud, as a radio
15 Cawer
16 Let __ a secret
17 Write without a single mistake
20 Cosmonauts, by definition
21 Perfume essence
22 Phone no. at the office
23 Letters starting naval carrier names
25 With 28-Down, a university in Dixie
26 Cass Elliot was one of them
30 Watering holes
31 Kimono sashes
32 1961 Best Actor Maximilian
34 British rule in colonial India
37 Not play it safe
40 Ave. crossers
41 Nal, e.g., chemically
42 Poems of praise
43 Look surreptitiously
44 Search
45 Prefix with cycle
48 6-pt. scores
49 Sigma follower
51 Spotted pony
53 Sunrise and sunset locales
58 O.K.
61 Sea eagle
62 First number in season records
63 French pupil
64 High schooler

65 Like custards
66 Called one's bluff

DOWN

1 Shortened form, in shortened form
2 __ cheese dressing
3 Dutch artist Frans
4 Mined metals
5 Knots again
6 Bloodhound's trail
7 Goofs
8 Opposition for Dems.
9 Wonderment
10 Refine, as flour
11 "And __ grow on"
12 Hometown-related

13 __ nous
18 I.R.S.'s share
19 Grapple (with), colloquially
23 Overturn
24 Soothing ointment
26 Swabs
27 Adjoin
28 See 25-Across
29 Baseball wood
30 Valentino title role, with "the"
32 Covered the foot
33 Yields
34 Went on horseback
35 King Kong and others
36 It's said with a poke in the ribs
38 First-rate

39 Cardinals great Brock
44 In sets of 24 sheets
45 Come-from-behind victory
46 Saltpeter: Brit.
47 Silly
49 She said "I 'spect I growed"
50 Dadaism founder
52 Govt. agents
53 Be suspended
54 French novelist Émile
55 "Roger, __ and out!"
56 Central church area
57 Winter toy
59 Be indebted to
60 Not worth a __

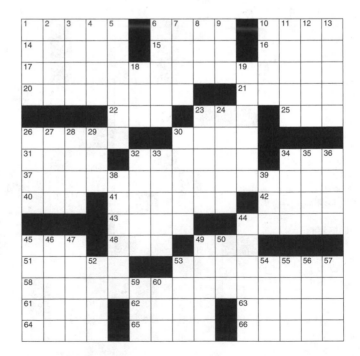

by Bill Ballard

ACROSS
1 Legally impedes
7 May school event, often
11 Like 1, 3 or 7
14 Filled with the old school spirit
15 The last Mrs. Chaplin
16 By way of
17 ST
20 Spreading tree
21 Legal offense
22 Main bloodline
23 Hair division
24 Pharmaceutical-approving org.
25 TU
33 Cut dramatically
34 Not quite closed
35 Life force, in Eastern philosophy
36 Luke's mentor, in "Star Wars"
37 Bombastic
39 Bunny's tail
40 When repeated, a dance
41 Bulging earthenware vessel
42 Legal setting
43 UV
47 Toward the tiller
48 Meadow murmurs
49 Jellied dish
52 Young seal
54 Sign of success
57 VW
60 Little ___, 60's singer
61 Disney's "___ of the South"
62 Runoff point
63 Actress Susan
64 Tarzan's home
65 Canine covering

DOWN
1 Highlands tongue
2 Political comic Mort
3 ___ McAn shoes
4 Hart Trophy winner, 1970–72
5 1987 Wimbledon winner
6 Steinhauer of the L.P.G.A.
7 Sonnet, e.g.
8 Teased mercilessly
9 Switch settings
10 El toro's opponent
11 Completed
12 Weight loss plan
13 Spreadsheet numbers
18 Silents star Naldi
19 Speckled horse
23 Leaning Tower's city
24 Come apart at the seams
25 Course in which to study Freud
26 Wahine's welcome
27 Kind of beacon
28 Like Fran Drescher's voice
29 What to wear when one goes beddy-bye
30 Come to pass
31 "Star Trek" lieutenant
32 ___-gritty
37 Overabundance
38 The whole enchilada
39 Drunkards
41 Thrown away
42 Johnny Appleseed's real surname
44 Seriously wound
45 "Yeah, sure!"
46 Aplenty
49 Like some cheddar cheese
50 P.G.A. Masters champion Ballesteros
51 Talk in church
52 Go downhill
53 Bigger than the both of us
54 Fat-free, as milk
55 Russo of "In the Line of Fire"
56 Hurler Hershiser
58 Neither's partner
59 Gardner of "The Barefoot Contessa"

by Raymond Hamel

6

ACROSS

1 Stamp apparatus
6 Macbeth, for one
11 Grp. concerned with genealogy
14 Fencing action
15 Mirage, maybe
16 Do, so to speak
17 Maces?
19 How most goods must be ordered by mail: Abbr.
20 Ivan and Nicholas
21 Tom Jones's love, in "Tom Jones"
23 Milk dispenser
25 Grayish-tan
28 __ empty stomach
29 Saharan
31 Be an A-one scout?
34 Doles (out)
36 What turns 19 into 21?
37 Office messages
40 Kind of shock
44 Spain's Princess __
46 "The Divine Comedy" poet
47 Patrick Ewing and Walt Frazier?
52 Animated character
53 Clara, e.g., on "Bewitched"
54 Linguini, for instance
56 It does blowups
57 Some guitars
60 Feature of many letters
62 Latish lunchtime
63 Toured Great Britain extensively?
68 When Thanksgiving is celebrated in Can.
69 Taken for granted
70 Wickerwork twig
71 Parisian possessive
72 Ohio, e.g.
73 Belated

DOWN

1 Type
2 Resident of St. Mary's
3 Clever seamstresses?
4 __ Benedict
5 "Get clean" program
6 Alarm
7 "2001" computer
8 Tempe sch.
9 Penpoints
10 Classic gas brand
11 Nymph loved by Apollo
12 Ancient Rome's __ Way
13 Household pest
18 Schlepp
22 Skunk
23 __ David
24 Nabisco treat
26 Word on all U.S. coins
27 Flock members
30 Picks up
32 Egyptian boy king
33 LSD
35 Lingerie material
38 Gymnast's goal
39 Fastener
41 Rope-tying exhibition?
42 Harrow's rival
43 Monthly check
45 Dr.'s org.
47 Bomb sound
48 Subtlety
49 Map features
50 Ancient Palestinian
51 Submachine gun
55 Lingo
58 E.R. helps
59 Tiff
61 Ingrid's role in "Casablanca"
64 Perón of Argentina
65 Like April weather
66 Nancy Drew's boyfriend
67 Not like April weather

by Randall J. Hartman

ACROSS

1 Presidential caucus state
5 Relax
9 "The __ Ranger"
13 Some of it is junk
14 Go __ detail
15 Rescued
16 French 101 infinitive
17 Croaker
18 Revise
19 1986 Newman/ Cruise movie
22 Site of a ship's controls
23 Debtor's note
24 One-named co-star of "Jingle All the Way"
28 Chaos
32 Like a stadium crowd
33 Stewpot
35 __ Grande
36 Cynical foreign policy
40 Earnings on a bank acct.
41 Lemon and lime drinks
42 Commie
43 Sites of lashes
46 Pressure
47 "Are you a man __ mouse?"
48 Landlocked African country
50 "Fiddler" refrain
58 Up and about
59 TV's talking horse
60 Comfort
61 Fred's dancing partner
62 Not yours
63 Cake finisher
64 Carol
65 Picnic invaders
66 Library byword

DOWN

1 "__ a man with seven wives"
2 Sworn word
3 Telegram
4 Actor Guinness
5 Ransacked
6 Register, as for a course
7 Tempest
8 Like some restaurant orders
9 Hope/Crosby co-star Dorothy
10 Kiln
11 State bird of Hawaii
12 Whirlpool
15 Pago Pago's land

20 John who wrote "Butterfield 8"
21 Last
24 "Sexy" lady of Beatles song
25 Certain humor
26 Actor Nick
27 __ Harbour, Fla.
28 Swiss heights
29 Construction site sight
30 Rubes
31 They're used in walking the dog
33 Bettor's stat
34 Golf position
37 Traffic tool
38 Kind of nerve
39 Russian space station
44 Massachusetts city
45 "Goodnight" girl of song

46 Playground equipment
48 California county
49 "__ You Glad You're You?" (1945 hit)
50 Persia, today
51 Pooch's name
52 "Gotcha"
53 Austen heroine
54 Legatee
55 Riot spray
56 Sailing
57 Uncool sort

by Sheldon Benardo

8

ACROSS

1 Front-line chow, once
5 Observer
10 Neighbor of Libya
14 Ear part
15 Fall color
16 In vigorous health
17 Scores on a serve
18 1996 film for which Geoffrey Rush won Best Actor
19 Chester Arthur's middle name
20 Start of a thought by Oscar Wilde
23 Neither's partner
24 Good Housekeeping award
25 Diddley and Derek
28 From the jungle
31 Brew vessels
35 Conductor Klemperer
37 Cozy corner
39 Iron bar
40 Part 2 of the thought
43 New Testament king
44 Flute part
45 Part of Q.E.D.
46 "Gunsmoke" star
48 Back-to-school mo.
50 Peter, Paul and Mary: Abbr.
51 Sleep phenomena
53 Flight
55 End of the thought
63 Up to it
64 Followed a coxswain's orders
65 Kind of miss
66 Safe deposit box item, perhaps
67 Witch
68 Great-great-grandson of Augustus
69 When the French fry?
70 Carved
71 Annexes

DOWN

1 Wooden piece
2 Little of Verdi?
3 Genesis brother
4 A quark and an antiquark
5 90's fashion accessory
6 ___ Rios, Jamaica
7 Waiflike
8 Birds at sea
9 Brand of peanut butter cup
10 Dare
11 Fair share, maybe
12 Jai ___
13 Game rooms
21 "I'll never do it again," e.g.
22 Dine at home
25 South African politico
26 Multiple-choice answer
27 Unsmiling
29 Clark's interest
30 Do's and ___
32 Stravinsky et al.
33 Yogurt type
34 R.B.I.'s and such
36 Wind player's purchases
38 Locale for a spanking
41 Ford flub
42 Blew inward
47 Buss
49 Scot's topper
52 Entrap
54 Food from heaven
55 Stow, as cargo
56 Sarcastic response
57 ___ Bailey
58 Increase
59 Québec's Lévesque
60 "___ I say more?"
61 Joker, e.g.
62 Love's inspiration

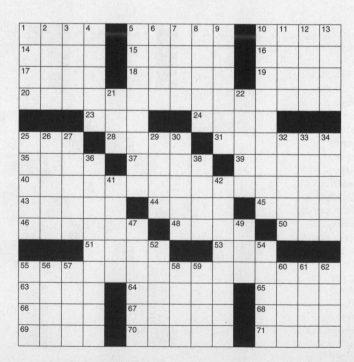

by Elizabeth C. Gorski

ACROSS

1 Suffered terribly
5 Spicy stew
9 Jean-Luc's father
13 Remorseful one
14 Witch's ride
15 VIII × VIII
16 Lube job supply
18 Cathedral nook
19 Do an impression of
20 One who's coming out
21 Uno + dos
22 Early part of a race?
26 Whitewater enthusiast
28 Classic theater name
29 Suffix with eye or ear
31 Elvis's "___ Not You"
32 Cockpit abbr.
33 Leg-puller
35 Sci-fi writer Card
38 Jetsam of 1773
39 Wifely
41 6, on a phone
42 Record holder?
44 Everybody's opposite
45 Aspiration
46 Squid's squirts
48 "Quincy, M.E." actor
49 Some sheets
50 Proposal
52 Girded (oneself)
54 Name of 12 popes
55 Quirk
57 Babe
58 Asia's Trans ___ mountain range
59 Sight in an intensive care unit
64 Jazzman Stan
65 Pure-and-simple
66 Eavesdrop
67 ___ Stanley Gardner
68 The enemy
69 New Age music superstar

DOWN

1 Flammable 60's item
2 Neighbor of Ger.
3 Slithery swimmer
4 Visionary
5 Band of gold?
6 Heap (on)
7 Not a medalist
8 They have pseudopods
9 LP
10 Alternative to special delivery
11 Former sleeper
12 Preholiday nights
14 Uncle Remus character
17 Phi Beta Kappa concern, for short
22 Talk, talk, talk
23 Popular watch
24 Volcano southeast of Mexico City
25 Sgt. Preston's home
27 Cello feature
30 The king of France
33 Hong Kong sights
34 Takes to the streets
36 Temporarily put aside
37 Wanderer
40 Bar request
43 It fits all, in a phrase
47 Not participate in
49 Crème de ___
50 Mason, at times
51 Beethoven's "Pastoral" Symphony
53 One billion years
54 Bellhop
56 Cellular suffix
60 Solitaire
61 Though, poetically
62 House vote
63 Singer's syllable

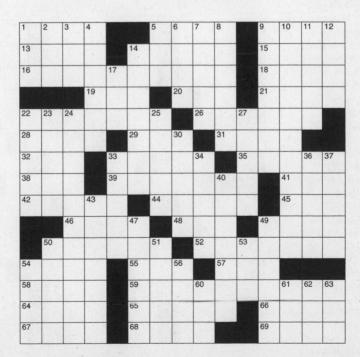

by Sam Bellotto Jr.

ACROSS

1 "Hey, Mac!"
5 Nautical pole
9 Home of Iowa State
13 Bank take-back
14 Vacation destination, with "the"
15 Diminished by
16 Author ___ S. Connell
17 Vicksburg lithographs?
19 ___-de-lance
20 Goes phhht!
21 List recipient
22 Jonesboro metal worker?
25 Conductor Zubin
27 Israel ___ (Irving Berlin, originally)
28 Yodeler's perch
30 Brit. lexicon
31 Positive reply to an invitation
32 Ed.'s request
34 To boot
35 Oak Ridge highway posting?
38 Peppy
41 Cheat, in a way
42 Sahara rarity
45 Stella D'___ (cookie name)
46 Tic-tac-toe win
47 Cool treat
49 "Peanuts," e.g.
51 Erie lighthouse locale?
54 African tribesman
56 "Hurry up and ___"
57 When doubled, a Thor Heyerdahl title
58 Mystic painter?
60 In the thick of
61 Erstwhile
62 Rest room sign
63 Construction wood
64 One on the go
65 Irascible
66 M.I.T. grads

DOWN

1 Ready-made
2 Unspecified number
3 Champagnes do this
4 Whole bunch
5 Shrank (from)
6 Group whose work is picking up
7 Horace's "___ Poetica"
8 Bench-press iterations
9 Dress cut
10 Vicks VapoRub ingredient
11 Ritzy homes
12 Conscription org.
14 Photog's request
18 Water-skier's apparatus
20 None too brainy
23 Quick with the comebacks
24 Like W.C. Fields's voice
26 ___ Annie, of "Oklahoma!"
29 Annie ___, Enoch Arden's wife
32 Busybody
33 Cleo's undoing
34 Hersey locale
36 Sgt., for one
37 Explode
38 Leftist label: Abbr.
39 Without compensation
40 Woo
43 1970's despot
44 City on the Yangtze
46 Prefix with -gon
47 Fits of anger
48 Piano school assignments
50 Word with city or circle
52 The "E." in A.E.S.
53 Unpleasant, as weather
55 Importune
58 Package letters
59 Dancer Shawn
60 Goon

by Fred Piscop

ACROSS

1 Polish's partner
5 Silents actress Normand
10 Disappearing phone feature
14 Busy person's list heading
15 "The Barber of Seville," e.g.
16 Loafing
17 Dreadful end
18 Hornswoggle
19 Butcher's stock
20 Short-lived success
23 Skull
24 Building wing
25 Skirt fold
28 Second-stringer
31 Command to Bowser
35 Windpipe, e.g.
37 Spigot
39 Not worth a ___
40 Backstabber
44 6–3, in tennis
45 Letter before "cue"
46 Forewarns
47 Crumble, as support
50 Any planet
52 Analyze
53 "Independence Day" invaders
55 Farm fraction
57 Old fogy
63 Trendy
64 Die down
65 Sombrero feature
67 One of six for a hexagon
68 X, mathwise
69 Liquid rock
70 Profess
71 Perfect places
72 Enthusiasm

DOWN

1 The usual: Abbr.
2 [It's gone!]
3 False god
4 Hiawatha's weapon
5 Coffee shop order
6 Plant pests
7 Existed
8 The "E" in Q.E.D.
9 Carpenter's machine
10 Feature of a baby face
11 The very notion
12 TV's Thicke
13 "___ Me Call You Sweetheart"
21 Caterpillar hairs
22 North Pole toymaker
25 Old hat
26 The Titanic, e.g.
27 Muse of poetry
29 Out-and-out
30 Old-fashioned "Phooey!"
32 Russian royals
33 ___ Rica
34 Impudent girl
36 Kennel sound
38 Black-eyed ___
41 Prefix with colonial
42 Blinding light
43 Look like
48 Salt, e.g.
49 And so on, for short
51 Close securely, with "down"
54 Rollerblade
56 Deep Blue's game
57 Switchblade
58 Ocean motion
59 Footnote abbr.
60 Christen
61 Russia's ___ Mountains
62 Beverly Sills, e.g.
63 Civil War letters
66 Million ___ March

by Gregory E. Paul

12

ACROSS
1 Arctic dweller
5 Cuneiform stroke
10 "Pronto!"
14 Treaty signer
15 About the line of rotation
16 200-meter, e.g.
17 Onetime feminine ideal
20 Big chunk of a drug company's budget
21 Golf's __ Cup
22 Same old, same old
23 Release money
25 Strait of Dover port
29 Novelty singing feature
33 Modern surveillance tool
34 Actress Winslet
35 Certain theater, for short
36 1941 Lillian Hellman play
40 Barely make, with "out"
41 Wine sediment
42 Big name in stationery
43 Insane
46 Incenses
47 Filly, e.g.
48 "What's more . . ."
49 __ Park, N.J.
52 Sun circler
57 Anthony Burgess thriller, with "A"
60 Et __
61 Foreign
62 Nonplus
63 Emperor in "Quo Vadis?"
64 Primed
65 After-dinner drink

DOWN
1 Cowardly Lion portrayer
2 Cream ingredient
3 "Not only that . . ."
4 Combustible pile
5 Bewhiskered creature
6 On the money
7 Menu offering
8 Xenon, for one
9 Pixie
10 Having a diamond-shaped pattern
11 50's–60's Mideast king
12 A lot of lot
13 Equal
18 Showy
19 Showy flower
23 Spa
24 On the sheltered side
25 Sounded crowlike
26 Suffering from insomnia
27 Subsequently
28 N.C. State's athletic org.
29 Doomed
30 Stale
31 Drift
32 Uncaps
34 Prepare to be knighted
37 Gymnast Korbut
38 Provide
39 Witch
44 1955 merger
45 Out-of-the-way place
46 "Friends, Romans, countrymen" orator
48 Begged
49 Shoemaker Thom
50 Lui's partner
51 Film __
52 Song for Carmen
53 Hoof smoother
54 Aware of
55 Helicopter pioneer Sikorsky
56 Educ. or H.U.D., e.g.
58 Gulf __
59 Ring cheer

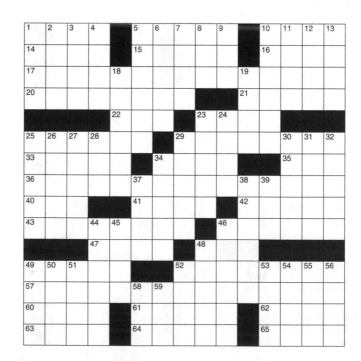

by Arthur S. Verdesca

ACROSS

1 Mah-jongg piece
5 "Saved by the ___!"
9 Het up
14 Declare
15 "Garfield" dog
16 Confused struggle
17 Small skirt
18 Chew like a beaver
19 Perfect
20 North Dakota tourist attraction
23 Building annex
24 Attack
25 Campus military org.
27 "Auf wiedersehen" wisher
31 Gymnast Korbut
34 Indian prince
38 Facility
39 British pound, informally
40 To the left side of a ship
41 Fleur-de-___
42 Good ol' boy's nickname
43 Comedian Danny of "The Court Jester"
44 Run pledges through the gantlet, say
45 Positive replies
46 Isle of exile for Napoleon
47 English cathedral city
49 ___-friendly
51 Neighborhood
56 Show ___ (Hollywood and such)
58 Fatty bulges
62 Seeped
64 "I smell ___!"

65 Nonglass parts of glasses
66 Martin or McQueen
67 Position
68 Woodwind
69 Person who gives a hoot
70 Miffed, with "off"
71 Neighbor of Wis.

DOWN

1 Home of the Buccaneers
2 Wall-climbing plants
3 Horne and Olin
4 Writer Jong
5 Stupefy
6 Poet ___ St. Vincent Millay
7 Tall tale teller

8 Bawdy
9 Certain acid
10 Homer Simpson's neighbor
11 Singing groups
12 Not imaginary
13 Cry
21 Pieces of ___
22 Sea eagle
26 Brimless hat
28 Kick back
29 Indian corn
30 Good thing to have
32 Barbed remark
33 Nabokov heroine and others
34 Gather leaves
35 "Be ___!" ("Help me out!")
36 Prankster's item
37 Zones

42 Poet who originated the phrase " truth is stranger than fiction"
44 Submarine
48 Thrilled to death
50 Church V.I.P.
52 Modern multimedia tool
53 Accused's need
54 Wretched car
55 City on the Ruhr
56 Popular pear
57 Infinitesimal amount
59 Infinite
60 Lake that feeds Niagara Falls
61 Abhor
63 Apple picker

by Shannon Burns

14

ACROSS

1 Automobile pioneer
5 Baby's affliction
10 Sailing maneuver
14 Pub missile
15 "Is that ___?" ("Really?")
16 Precollege, briefly
17 Military attire
19 Iranian money
20 Reggae relative
21 Yarn maker
22 Troutlike fish
23 Plants with small, fragrant flowers
27 Kind of lantern
29 Playwright O'Casey
30 Masters and Jonson, e.g.
31 Pellet propeller
35 Jerk
36 ___ the good
38 Sportscaster Berman
39 One of the Virgin Islands
42 On the ___ (not working)
44 Sign
45 Go along with
47 Leafy dish
51 Willow twig
52 One of the "back 40"
53 Motorists' org.
56 "Scat, cat!"
57 Breakfast side dish
60 Computer list
61 Cow of note
62 Anniversary, e.g.
63 Kiln
64 Check writer
65 Potato features

DOWN

1 Lotto info
2 Escapade
3 Most marvelous
4 Ave. crossers
5 Mountain retreats
6 Recently
7 Actress San Giacomo
8 Diamonds, to a yegg
9 Pennies: Abbr.
10 End points
11 1979 sci-fi classic
12 Classroom supply
13 Glasgow garb
18 Turns sharply
22 Fight, but not for real
24 It borders four Great Lakes: Abbr.
25 "___ me?"
26 Pianist Peter
27 Calculating types
28 Welcomer
31 Capp and Capone
32 Takes to the air
33 Riga native
34 Auto maker Ferrari
36 New World abbr.
37 Get, as a job
40 Finish putting
41 Bridge expert Sharif
42 Less restrained
43 Cartoon canine
45 Comic strip redhead
46 Big name in baby food
47 Kramer of "Seinfeld"
48 Actor Milo
49 Club members since 1917
50 Given to gabbing
54 What's required to be "in"
55 "___ Death" (Grieg work)
57 Wise
58 It goes before carte, but not horse
59 Keats creation

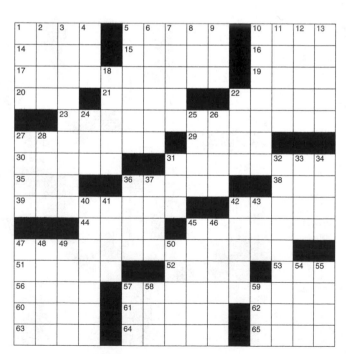

by Rich Norris

ACROSS

1 Liberal follower
5 Help with the dishes
9 Frontier dwelling
14 Orderly
15 The old sod
16 Small type
17 Ironed?
19 Brewing need
20 U.F.O. crew
21 Hoodwink
23 Barrel parts
25 Lightweight hat
29 Back biter
31 Wacky
33 Fastidious
36 Wrinkled?
38 Nile slitherer
39 Ann and May
40 Noted twin
41 Extinguished?
44 X-rated
46 Nonpointed end
47 Stable worker
49 It's often heard during storms
51 Baroque
54 Presuming that
56 Neighbor of Namibia
58 Provide funding for
62 Renounced?
64 Miss America topper
65 Bibliography abbr.
66 Hawaiian honker
67 Westminster, for one
68 Bank (on)
69 Those muchachas

DOWN

1 Time ___ half
2 Holders of many frames
3 Implied
4 Fords are made here
5 Pop goer
6 Taxing letters
7 Pinto
8 Become, finally
9 ___ pepper
10 The time of one's life?
11 Flock sound
12 Part of T.G.I.F.
13 New Jersey pro
18 Representative
22 Skating event
24 Peace Nobelist of 1978
26 Dunderhead
27 Part of an atomic clock
28 With regard to
30 Replace a wooden pin
32 Irritable
33 Fall behind in the stretch
34 Spreadsheet workers
35 Relative of "thud"
37 "Don Quixote" role
39 O'Donnell of "Mad Love"
42 Book before Jeremiah: Abbr.
43 Brief vacation
44 Italian lady
45 John Lennon song
48 Viva voce
50 Beverage in a jug
52 Parts of "complete works"
53 "Maria ___" (1941 hit)
55 Bash
57 Citrus quaffs
58 Hellenic vowel
59 Pen point
60 Smidgen
61 Comstock output
63 Old White House nickname

by Richard Silvestri

16

ACROSS
1 Sound astonished
5 "Hound Dog" man
10 Chicken bite
14 "Tell __ My Heart" (1987 hit)
15 Nickels and dimes
16 Author Hunter
17 One who runs a jail?
19 Fiddler while Rome burned
20 Alpha's opposite
21 __ school (doctor's training)
22 Chronic nag
23 Twisty curve
24 Broach, as a subject
27 Toe woe
28 Direct path
32 Gas pump rating
35 Adds to the mixture
36 Undecided
37 Something to believe
39 "__ kleine Nachtmusik"
40 Overfrequently
42 TV's Greene and Michaels
44 Seasoned vets
45 Pianist Myra
46 First in time
48 Long time
51 Hardly any
54 Chicken __ king
55 Waned
57 Walk the waiting room
58 Sautéing, jail-style?
60 Partner of "done with"
61 Poke fun at
62 Singer Adams
63 Kennedy and Turner
64 Viper
65 Views

DOWN
1 Army figure
2 Parts of molecules
3 Hogs' homes
4 Ping-__
5 Environmentalist's prefix
6 One at the bottom of the totem pole
7 Grew like ivy
8 Worse than awful, foodwise
9 Kazakhstan, once: Abbr.
10 Jail cells?
11 Always
12 Give a hoot
13 Have memorized
18 Hawk's grabber
22 British submachine gun
25 __ Set (kid's builder)
26 Pokes fun at
27 Jail keys?
29 "The doctor __"
30 Prime time hour
31 Chemical endings
32 Director Preminger
33 Groovy
34 Tramped (on)
35 London's Big __
38 Put back on the agenda
41 "Animal House" grp.
43 Blender maker
45 Final transport
47 Story of Achilles
48 Put up with
49 Magical wish granter
50 Noses (out)
51 TV commercial
52 Bat's home
53 Scored 100 on
56 Tournament passes
58 Train terminal: Abbr.
59 Not agin

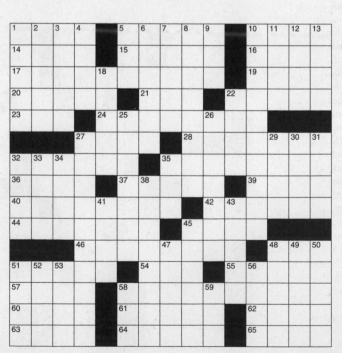

by Nancy Salomon

ACROSS

1 Carpenter's gadget
6 XXXI times V
9 Hardly spine-tingling
13 Express again
14 China's Chou En-___
15 Capital NW of Twin Falls
16 With 58-Across, a classic line associated with 47-Across
19 Ethel Waters's "___ Blue?"
20 Concert equipment
21 Apprehensively
22 Oscar-winning actor in 47-Across
26 Hope is here: Abbr.
27 Automne preceder
28 "Indubitably"
31 Coeur d' ___, Idaho
34 "Your Erroneous Zones" author Wayne
35 I.B.M., e.g.
36 Kind of wagon
38 Section of Queens, N.Y.
40 Yard tool
41 Like ___ out of hell
43 Church cries
44 Wks. and wks.
45 Baby blossom
46 "We ___ the World"
47 Oscar-winning film
53 Inflationary path
56 Inlet
57 Lyric poem
58 See 16-Across

62 Seal fur trader
63 Boeing 737, e.g.
64 Window parts
65 Pioneer's heading
66 Hit show sign
67 Confuse

DOWN

1 "Iliad" king
2 Auxiliary proposition
3 Allegheny's successor
4 Steamed
5 "Ciao!"
6 What clematis plants do
7 Slippery one
8 Rome's Appia or Veneto
9 Like some B'way performances
10 Biography
11 On the main
12 München mister
15 Link
17 Bit of yarn
18 Frisco gridders
23 Arm of a knight-in-arms
24 Snack that's bitten or licked
25 Corroded
28 Time long past
29 Leprechauns' land
30 Get-well spots
31 Out of whack
32 Limerick maker
33 Lodge fellows
34 Fix a computer program
35 Doomsday cause, maybe
37 Old phone company sobriquet

39 Skater Lipinski
42 Embellisher
46 Many miles away
47 Rainbow ___
48 ___ monde (society)
49 "Same here"
50 Keep after
51 Eponym for failure
52 Dodger Hall-of-Famer
53 "Pygmalion" writer
54 Soccer superstar
55 Boardwalk refreshments
59 Spinners' spinners?
60 Pollution stds. setter
61 Tattoos, currently

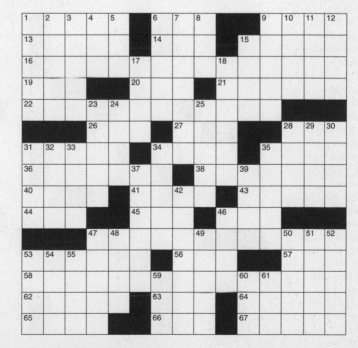

by Bill Ballard

18

ACROSS

1 Take five
5 Engineers' schools, for short
10 Neighbor of Sudan
14 "If __ I should leave . . ."
15 Musical key
16 Freight car hopper
17 Thackeray novel
19 Plunders
20 Pristine
21 Like some bank checking
22 Quito-to-Rio dir.
23 Sprout
24 Early offspring
26 Newspaper bigwigs
31 Copyists
34 Test for a college sr.
35 Clip chaser
36 Russian river
38 Ethical standards
39 Kind of land
40 Vittles
41 Information from tree rings
42 Uses a darning egg
43 Lowbrow talk-show guest, maybe
47 Remain
48 Phone stand item
49 Peanut butter brand
52 Suggest
55 North Dakota neighbor
57 Mathematician Turing
58 Symbol of virility
60 Glue
61 Lover
62 Drinks at the Pink Pig, say
63 Is looking tired
64 Goes downhill
65 "This __ laughing matter!"

DOWN

1 Casino show
2 Olympian Janet
3 Intuit
4 Beethoven's "Archduke __"
5 Fortensky's ex
6 Decadent
7 Attired
8 "Bali __"
9 The Bosporus, e.g.: Abbr.
10 Biographer
11 Hard thing to walk on?
12 French cleric
13 Two tablets, maybe
18 __ Andronicus
21 Wellness org.
24 Treat successfully
25 Some 120 m.p.h. serves
26 They toot their own horns
27 Get to yes
28 Verve
29 Do origami
30 Bath add-ons
31 60's British P.M. Douglas-Home
32 Fruit cooked in cream and sugar
33 Within: Prefix
37 Grp. advocating tough liquor laws
38 Brute
42 Emergency worker
44 Order to Fido
45 Let off
46 Some VCR's
49 Actor Grey and others
50 Dramatist Henrik
51 1980 DeLuise film
52 Talks one's ear off
53 Lamb alias
54 Ersatz juice
55 He's not one to talk
56 Spicy cuisine
58 Time divs.
59 Chat room inits.

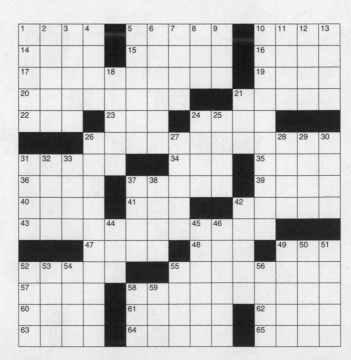

by Elizabeth C. Gorski

ACROSS

1 Feudal workers
6 Italian money, formerly
10 Con artist's art
14 Characteristic
15 Scent
16 Barbershop emblem
17 Indy 500 competitor
18 Suckling spot
19 Landed (on)
20 First step for a would-be groom vis-à-vis his intended's father
23 Director Craven
24 Mauna __
25 Arrow's path
26 New Deal org.
29 Kind of talk the would-be bride had with mom
32 Commedia dell'__
35 A.F.L.'s partner
36 __ into holy matrimony
37 Sets of pews
38 Namely
41 "__ pin and pick it up . . ."
42 Bullwinkle, e.g.
44 Opposite of WSW
45 Coffee servers
46 How the would-be groom proposed
50 Actor Fernando
51 Wedding __
52 Letters on a Cardinal's cap
53 Shoot the breeze
56 What the bride's father did vis-à-vis the reception
60 "Neato!"

62 Director Kazan
63 Kind of lily
64 Dull sound
65 Notes after do
66 Ebb and neap, e.g.
67 Peeved
68 British gun
69 What italics do

DOWN

1 Scarecrow stuffing
2 Wipe out
3 Pool ball sorters
4 Where 1-Across slaved
5 Golf shot
6 Ladies' man
7 __ fixe
8 Greet with loud laughter

9 Prefix with -pod or -scope
10 Bridge unit
11 It's thrown on bad ideas
12 He K.O.'d Foreman 10/30/74
13 Bumped into
21 Take countermeasures
22 Be in pain
27 Groom carefully
28 Gillette razors
29 "Siddhartha" writer
30 Hauled
31 Follow as a result
32 Knight's garb
33 TV news exec Arledge
34 Common board size

39 Tough job for a dry cleaner
40 Tithe amount
43 Within: Prefix
47 Library gadgets
48 Shoelace hole
49 Votes into office
53 Funny lady Radner
54 Funny man Woody
55 Great time, or great noise
57 Kind of shoppe
58 Onetime phone call cost
59 Get-out-of-jail money
60 Pennies: Abbr.
61 "Well, what's this?!"

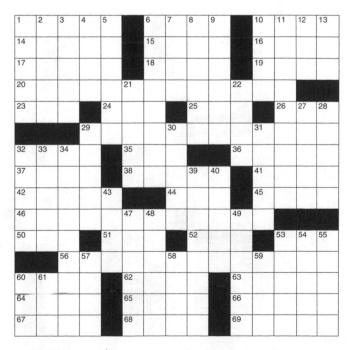

by Mark Danna

ACROSS

1 Chair part
5 Stuff
9 Blackmore heroine Lorna
14 Salon focus
15 Capital of Latvia
16 Writer Sinclair
17 Meat inspection inits.
18 Journey for Caesar
19 5 to 1, say
20 Best Picture of 1987
23 Der ___ (Adenauer)
24 Malt kiln
25 Neighbor of Chile: Abbr.
28 Woodlands
30 Actress Novak
33 "Vive ___ !" (old French cry)
35 Truman's nuclear agcy.
36 Grandma, affectionately
37 Opera by Glinka
41 Others
42 Furrow
43 Nutso
44 Encountered
45 Educator Mary McLeod ___
48 Fifth quarters, so to speak: Abbr.
49 Rip
50 Pres. Reagan and others
52 Popular dish often served with rice
58 Shoot at, as tin cans
59 Excellent
60 Getting ___ years
61 Mooch
62 The "brains" of 58-Down
63 "___ girl!"

64 Saccharine
65 Pianist Myra
66 Missing

DOWN

1 Closed
2 Eye swatter?
3 White House staffer
4 Cheery song syllables
5 "The Count of Monte ___"
6 Singing cowboy Tex
7 Pulitzer writer James
8 Squirrellike monkey
9 Compulsion by force
10 Some 60's paintings

11 Germany's ___ von Bismarck
12 Roulette bet
13 Rock's Brian
21 1966 movie or song hit
22 Quilt part
25 Car protector
26 U.S. Grant opponent
27 Mill fodder
29 Astronauts' returning point
30 Musical toy
31 Unfitting
32 "The Bells of St. ___"
34 Frequently
36 Sgt., e.g.
38 Carnival oddity
39 Community service program

40 "Maria ___" (1941 hit song)
45 St. Thomas who was murdered in a cathedral
46 Seventh planet
47 Surprisingly
49 Slight color
51 Toast
52 Lobster pincer
53 Cover up
54 Slangy denial
55 Engrossed by
56 Pesky insects
57 Pesky insect
58 Modern office staples, for short

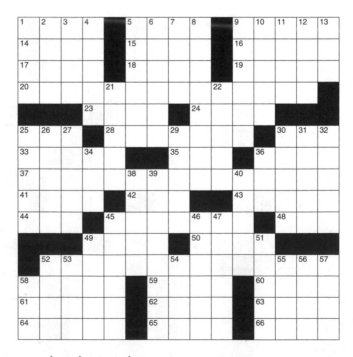

by Arthur S. Verdesca

ACROSS

1 Portend
5 Shopaholic's watchword
10 Small denomination
14 Sorority letters
15 Trial's partner
16 "Oh, were it not true!"
17 Gershwin's "It ___ Necessarily So"
18 1911 Stravinsky ballet
20 Flirt
22 Blacker
23 Short-lived Egypt-Syria union: Abbr.
24 O.E.D. item
25 Lands on the Persian Gulf
30 After-exercise refreshers
34 Having a pallor
35 Choir voice
37 Batter's woe
38 Roxy Music co-founder
39 1841 Adam ballet
41 Chinese "way"
42 Nostalgic look
44 Mozart's "Il mio tesoro," e.g.
45 Tart
46 Unbending
48 Chopin specialty
50 Keats's "To Autumn," e.g.
51 Altar in the sky
52 It's south of the Pyrenees
55 Family reunion activity
60 1945 Prokofiev ballet
62 Kan. neighbor
63 Head start
64 Actress Patricia et al.
65 Camera part
66 Dak., once
67 Kind of fund
68 Quod ___ faciendum

DOWN

1 Bric-a-___
2 Oberlin locale
3 1869 Minkus ballet
4 River's end
5 Important school mo.
6 ___-à-porter (ready-to-wear)
7 Highly collectible lithographer
8 Neither's partner
9 "Star Wars" characters
10 Amount Santa carries
11 Like some textbook publishing
12 Party centerpiece
13 Peter, e.g.
19 Misgiving
21 Cause that NOW championed
25 Decorative pitchers
26 "Le Déjeuner sur l'herbe" painter
27 ___ chi ch'uan
28 Forbidden-question asker, in "Lohengrin"
29 Rear
31 1892 Tchaikovsky ballet, with "The"
32 With all one's might
33 Some fine porcelain
36 Hodgepodge
39 Hawn of Hollywood
40 "Le ___ des cygnes"
43 Stock up on again
45 Halo
47 Longs (for)
49 Check
52 80's–90's hip-hop star
53 Wait
54 Technician: Abbr.
55 Blue, in Bonn
56 Shakespeare title starter
57 Reckless
58 It parallels a radius
59 90 degrees
61 Mud ___

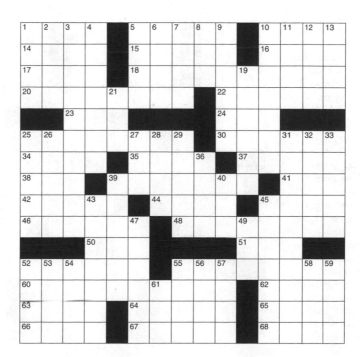

by Nancy S. Ross

ACROSS

1 Total
4 Castle protector
8 Sipper's aid
13 "___ tu" (Verdi aria)
14 Open, as a gate
16 Rapid-fire
17 Beavers' project
18 Former Bangkok-based grp.
19 Yens
20 Question of understanding, to a Spanish count?
23 Undemanding, as a job
24 Recede
25 "___ girl watcher" (1968 song lyric)
28 Actor Morales
29 Plant again
32 Boast
33 "The Old Wives' Tale" dramatist George
35 "Ars Poetica" poet
37 What a doctor prescribes, to a Spanish count?
40 Lacking interest
41 "Same here"
42 Harvest
43 Important element of rap lyrics
45 Where baby sleeps
49 ___ Lanka
50 Coffee alternative
51 Alan Ladd western
52 Minute nutritional components, to a Spanish count?
56 Former House Majority Leader
59 Cease-fire
60 Cause for a Band-Aid
61 Perjurers
62 Swashbuckling Flynn
63 Word repeated in "takes ___ to know ___"
64 Slight contamination
65 Mailed
66 Bloodshot

DOWN

1 Tempt
2 Planet beyond Saturn
3 Brunch drink
4 Like cooked oatmeal
5 Prime draft classification
6 Blind as ___
7 Jacques of French cinema
8 Edible pigeon
9 Swirl
10 Trucker's truck
11 Serve that zings
12 Divs. of months
15 He was asked "Wherefore art thou?"
21 Creates quickly
22 "Charlotte's Web" author
25 Shah's land, once
26 Anti-attacker spray
27 "___ before beauty"
29 "Foul!" caller
30 Shade provider
31 Rundown
32 Sweet roll
34 Long, long time
36 World Series mo.
37 Stags and does
38 Town east of Santa Barbara
39 Barely lit
40 P.S.A.T. takers
44 Swiftness
46 Ill will
47 What musical instruments should be
48 Defeated
50 Rendezvous
51 Relative of the salmon
52 Graceful aquatic bird
53 Goes astray
54 Tempt
55 Supply-and-demand subj.
56 Not the main route: Abbr.
57 Narrow inlet
58 ___ tai

by Evie Eysenburg

ACROSS

1 Won't-keep-you-up-at-night beverage
6 Improvisation
11 Hon
14 Beethoven dedicatee
15 The supreme Supreme
16 Simile's center
17 Not discreet
19 Rendezvoused
20 Mekong River land
21 English university city
23 Fixes securely
27 Morsel
29 Whole
30 Kind of microscope
33 Plucked instruments
34 Put (down), as money
35 Power serve, perhaps
36 London "stops"
37 Rounded the edges of
38 Catcher's catcher
39 Advice giver Landers
40 Fragrant trees
41 French legislature
42 Portions
44 Word before Highness
45 Not in port
46 Broke off (from)
47 Poem
49 Portion
50 Video maker, for short
51 Hardly generous
58 Numbered rd.
59 Up ___ (stuck)
60 Maine university town
61 Frowning

62 Puts in an overhead compartment, say
63 Three trios

DOWN

1 Dover's state: Abbr.
2 "Do Ya" group, for short
3 A.F.L.-___
4 Dummkopf
5 They're put out at times
6 "See ya!"
7 Ballroom dance maneuvers
8 Napkin's place
9 Like Bach's Violin Sonata No. 3
10 Casino affliction
11 Not too smart
12 Preowned

13 Chocolate factory sights
18 Highway division
22 C.P.R. expert
23 "You guys . . ."
24 "Tennis, ___?"
25 Bullied
26 Father's Day favorites
27 This puzzle has 78
28 Tear apart
30 Some fashion magazines
31 Gas rating
32 Snared
34 One of Columbus's ships
37 Rare-coin rating
38 French mother
40 Old Madrid money
41 Arrondissement, in Paris

43 Holyoke and Sinai, e.g.: Abbr.
44 Slave
46 Fills up
47 Some RCA products
48 "I could ___ horse!"
49 Piano mover's cry
52 Blue chip giant
53 Miracle-___ (garden brand)
54 Sold-out inits.
55 Heavy weight
56 Atlanta-to-Raleigh dir.
57 Part of an E-mail address

by Elizabeth C. Gorski

ACROSS

1 Be wide open
5 Square fare?
9 Common alias
14 Port of "The Plague"
15 Tickle Me doll
16 Capital west of Haiphong
17 Like jokers, often
18 Steal a pass?
20 Formidable foe
22 Newcastle's river
23 Atty.-to-be exams
24 Lifesaving equipment
25 Popular cooking spray
28 Word said with a wave of the hand
30 Fabulous fur
32 Paving stuff
34 Unruly crowd
36 Swenson of "Benson"
37 For the birds?
39 Tabard Inn order
40 Understood
41 Big name in electronics
42 Beethoven's Third
44 "Get your hands off me!"
45 A wink or a nod, say
47 Pre-exercise exercise
49 Baseball's Kranepool and others
50 Spare, e.g.
52 Bobbing object
54 "Scram!"
55 Trap setters
57 Steal a novel?
61 "___ Camera"
62 Land of the Rising Sun
63 Philharmonic part
64 For men only
65 Sports data
66 Take care of
67 To be, in old Rome

DOWN

1 Dress for a ball
2 The Little Mermaid
3 Steal coils?
4 Make lovable
5 TV actress Gilbert
6 Yalies
7 Bowling alley initials
8 Game of chance
9 Fistfight result
10 Nutmeg-based spice
11 Old well's contents
12 Corn site
13 Smash
19 Melville tale
21 Rear
24 Steal from singer Nick?
25 Steal draperies?
26 1973 Rolling Stones #1 song
27 Substantial
29 Transportation on the slopes
31 Actress Farrow
32 Café cup
33 Skirt
35 "Star Wars" princess
38 Writer Rand
40 Buccaneers' bay
42 "A Cooking Egg" poet
43 Turned the handle
46 Parthenon's city
48 Revolt
51 "Lost in Space" figure
53 Bombeck and others
54 Card game played with sevens through aces
55 In a bit
56 Wise one
57 Bedwear, briefly
58 Horse's morsel
59 Tax preparer, for short
60 Medal bestowed by Eliz. II

by Karen Hodge

ACROSS

1 Essence
5 Fable finale
10 ___ facto
14 London district
15 Fruit container
16 See 47-Across
17 1944 Oscar-winning song by Bing Crosby
20 Jobs to do
21 Radiant
22 Inflation-fighting W.W. II org.
23 Vote of support
24 Actor Gibson
25 Years and years
27 Oats for horses, say
29 Hotel capacity
30 Commence
33 Pie ___ mode
34 Start of a counting-out rhyme
35 Like some Jewish delis
36 Berlin's home: Abbr.
37 Court divider
38 Like 10-watt bulbs
39 Friend in France
40 Not give up an argument
42 Spy's writing
43 Litter member
44 Japanese camera
45 Middle ears?
46 Church niche
47 With 16-Across, depressed
48 Doc bloc
49 Wield
50 Sure-footed work animal
52 Send, as money
54 Send elsewhere
57 1951 hit with music by former Veep Dawes

60 Christmastime
61 Go fishing
62 Tiptop
63 Soviet news agency
64 They're counted at meetings
65 See 45-Down

DOWN

1 "Hey there!"
2 Hawkeye State
3 1937 Benny Goodman hit
4 Reacted like a taxi driver?
5 Old Sprint rival
6 Embellish
7 Tattered
8 The Marshall Islands, e.g.
9 Jay who has Monday night "Headlines"

10 Conditions
11 1960 song from "Bye Bye Birdie"
12 Polaroid
13 Gumbo plant
18 Fed. property overseer
19 Stunning
26 Extra-play periods, for short
27 Dickens thief
28 1983 Nicholas Gage book
29 Red vegetable
31 Tale-spinning Uncle
32 Rubbish
34 Tangle up
35 Youngsters
38 Fight (with)
41 Charged particle
42 ___ and goings

45 With 65-Across, a Spanish highway
46 Sour brew
49 ___-Raphaelite
50 "It ___ pretty!"
51 Portico
53 Verve
55 Austen heroine
56 Stagger
58 Smith and Gore
59 "For ___ a jolly . . ."

by William Canine

ACROSS

1 Moby-Dick chaser
5 Hobble
9 Alternative if things don't work out
14 Vincent Lopez's theme song
15 Met highlight
16 Refuges
17 TV turner
18 Bridge, in Bretagne
19 Vowel sound
20 Modern times, to Auden
23 Paris airport
24 Stop __ dime
25 Nudge, as the memory
28 Copperhead's weapon
30 Snub, in a way
32 One of the Mrs. Sinatras
33 The 1890's, historically
37 Performing __
39 Acquire
40 Individuals
41 Sherlockian times
46 Scottish refusal
47 Chameleonlike creature
48 Confrere
50 Acquire, slangily
51 Explosive letters
53 Flabbergast
54 The 1980's, to yuppies
59 "East of Eden" director
62 Part of N.B.
63 Christiania, now
64 Brewer Samuel
65 Kind of proportions
66 __-mutton
67 Sioux dwelling
68 Smaller cousin of 67-Across
69 Expensive

DOWN

1 "Put Your Head on My Shoulder" singer
2 __ Kong
3 Tissue softener
4 Coarse dimwit
5 One of the Canary Islands
6 Often-missed humor
7 Impudent girl
8 Lanai
9 Stamps
10 Gossamer
11 Cigar leaving
12 Novel
13 Jamboree grp.
21 "Pennies __ Heaven"
22 Home of Phillips University
25 Actress Barnes or Kerns
26 Severe test
27 Skein formers
28 Ill-tempered woman
29 Devours
31 Cpl., e.g.
32 Like Mann's mountain
34 "That's awful!"
35 Dog doc
36 Summer on the Riviera
38 70's terrorist org.
42 Like some gazes
43 The Daltons, for example
44 Take back
45 Greenish-blue
49 Countless
52 Ism
53 Take effect
54 Broadway musical with the song "We Need a Little Christmas"
55 "Huh-uh"
56 "Things are becoming clear"
57 Masha and Irina's sister, in Chekhov
58 Queen of Jordan
59 Krazy __
60 Fruity quaff
61 Last sound some bugs hear

by Jonathan Schmalzbach

ACROSS

1 Problem in the defense lines
5 Mountain dew producer
10 Theories
14 On ___ with (equal to)
15 Lofty roost
16 Cannon of "Deathtrap"
17 First name in jeans
18 French and Indian War battle site
20 "Much Ado About Nothing" friar
22 Gallivant
23 Article in France-Soir
24 Clinton, e.g., before being Pres.
25 Igneous rock constituent
27 Grand Canyon view
31 It's 0 deg. at the equator
32 Pueblo material
33 With competence
35 Cause to grimace
39 Standard partner
40 "___ Man Answers" (1962 film)
41 "Pénélope" composer
42 "___ silly question . . ."
43 Recognize
44 Part of LEM
45 4, on a phone
47 Opened, as a door
49 "The Dating Game" contestant
53 Mentalist Geller
54 1-Down doubled
55 80's sitcom with the voice of Paul Fusco

56 Wild asses
60 Newfoundland's capital
63 Where Farsi is spoken
64 Shells and such
65 Standing by
66 "Lovely" Beatles girl
67 Arcing shots
68 Neighbor of Oman
69 Spring

DOWN

1 Soccer segment
2 Telephone abbr.
3 Kind of lamp
4 St. Patrick's Day phrase
5 Mouth moistener
6 They may be herbal

7 Tick off
8 Feudal lord
9 Under sanction
10 49-Across's last words
11 Vermont product
12 ___ cum laude
13 Vile smile
19 Classic Icelandic poetry
21 Nuclei
25 Quartet hidden in this puzzle
26 Beer brewed in Bremen
27 Hemingway's handle
28 Commotions
29 Breakfast area
30 Water source
34 Bowling green
36 Bee or Em

37 "Dies ___"
38 Disappointing date, maybe
41 Regional plants
43 Wet blanket
46 Qualifying race
48 Burner designer
49 Kind of metabolism
50 Texas shrine
51 Shinny
52 ___ mind (in agreement)
56 Story starter
57 Pelee Island's lake
58 Tat-tat preceder
59 Say with annoyance
61 Refusals
62 "She Done ___ Wrong"

by Mark Elliot Skolsky

ACROSS

1 Has speech difficulties
6 On ___ (like much freelance work)
10 Opera star
14 Brilliant success
15 Bathroom flooring
16 Japanese sashes
17 Diner offering
20 Hire
21 Partygoer
22 Shakespearean king
24 Historic periods
25 Walter Cronkite's network
28 Plant part
30 Amount eaten
34 The triple of a triple play
36 Org. overseeing fairness in hiring
38 Specified
39 Restaurant offering
42 Week or rear follower
43 Min. components
44 Author ___ Stanley Gardner
45 Emblems on Indian poles
47 Bucks' mates
49 Initials in fashion
50 In ___ land (dreaming)
52 "Three men in ___"
54 Living
58 Apache souvenirs
62 Lawn party offering
64 Sale caveat
65 Swallow
66 Emulate Cicero
67 Used E-mail
68 Verbally joust (with)
69 Continue a subscription

DOWN

1 ___-majesté
2 Computer signpost
3 False coin
4 Like John Paul II
5 Old Wells Fargo vehicles
6 Regular: Abbr.
7 Tower locale
8 Exhilarate
9 Prefix with -fugal
10 Like New York City, to Albany
11 Footnote abbr.
12 Bad habit, so to speak
13 Arthur ___ Stadium (U.S.T.A. facility)
18 Tidy up
19 Actress/singer Durbin
23 Marsh plants
25 Kitchen cleanser
26 It's good in Guadalajara
27 German city
29 Bike that zips in and out of traffic
31 Writer Cleveland ___
32 Starting points in shipbuilding
33 1950's Ford flop
35 Hardest and strongest
37 Drink with a marshmallow
40 Spanish fleet
41 Pesky African insect
46 Broken arm holders
48 Aid and comfort
51 Ending words in a price
53 Wilkes-___, Pa.
54 They were once "The most trusted name in television"
55 Facility
56 Injure, as a knee
57 ___ monster
59 Not having much fat
60 Cracker topping
61 Eurasian duck
63 Life-saving skill, for short

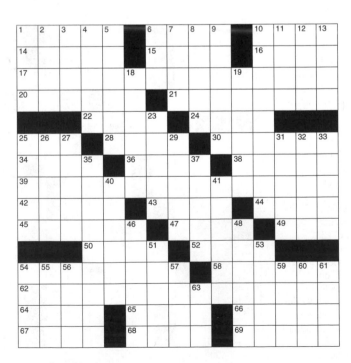

by Ed Early

ACROSS

1 Bay of Naples isle
6 Custard base
9 Hamburger, e.g.
14 Marriage
15 Word for
a superior
16 Nebraska's
biggest city
17 Pipe parts
18 Sports Illustrated's
1974 Sportsman
of the Year
19 Not so strict
20 "Impossible"
achievement
23 Poly-___
(college major)
24 Faux pas
25 Language
name suffix
28 Excise
30 Strikingly
unusual things
35 March
Madness org.
37 Offshore
apparatus
39 Prohibitions
for Junior
40 "Impossible"
discovery
44 Reach in amount
45 Parisian article
46 Toy on a string
47 Not always
50 Furry TV alien
52 Beachgoer's goal
53 Andy's boy,
in 60's TV
55 One of ___ own
57 "Impossible"
activity!
65 Angler of morays
66 Holm of
"Chariots of Fire"
67 More than some
68 Kind of acid
69 English ___
70 Goosebump-raising
71 Inner connection?

72 "Don't Bring Me
Down" rock grp.
73 Not neatniks

DOWN

1 Zodiacal
delineation
2 Get the pot going
3 Dock
4 Frolics
5 Bug
6 Birthright seller,
in Genesis
7 Poisonous desert
dwellers, for short
8 Radiator front
9 Sportsman's
mount
10 Amo, amas, ___
11 Curbside call
12 Lt. Kojak
13 Kitten's plaything
21 Pageant topper

22 Variety
25 Prefix with
structure
26 Reconnoiterer
27 Visit again
and again
29 Top of a
clock dial
31 Was in,
as a class
32 Eskimo
33 Terra ___
34 Visibly frightened
36 Voting "no"
38 African antelope
41 It's another day
42 Out ___ limb
43 One who
has life to look
forward to?
48 Smog-battling org.
49 Pretty as a
picture, e.g.

51 "Killing Me
Softly" pop
group, with "the"
54 Quick
communication
56 "Boléro" composer
57 They may be
strained in
young families
58 Do-___ (cabbage)
59 Actress Lena
60 Biological
trait carrier
61 Enjoying,
in slang
62 ___ Beach, Fla.
63 Tot's place
64 Whiskies

by William S. Cotter

30

ACROSS

1 Plays a round
6 U.S.A.F. NCO
10 Pianist Myra
14 Sanctuaries
15 Subscription length, often
16 Septi- plus one
17 Young pig
18 React to yeast
19 ___ Tower (San Francisco landmark)
20 Monkey business
22 Radius neighbor
23 Rajah's wife
24 Churchill's trademark
25 Beat to a pulp
29 Open, as a bag
31 Job for TV's Quincy
33 Oater settings
37 Hold gently
38 St. Thomas à ___ (martyred archbishop)
39 Hollow-eyed
41 Place
42 Safeguarded
44 Kind of analyst: Abbr.
45 Dangle a carrot in front of
48 They may be fair or square
50 Mélange
51 Chicken Little's friend
56 Look after
57 "Just ___!"
58 Say "fo'c's'le," for instance
59 Enthralled
60 Elephantine
61 ___ Highway (road through Ft. Nelson)
62 Orpheus' instrument
63 Greystoke's foster parents
64 Stinks to high heaven

DOWN

1 More than a scrape
2 Watchmen's watchdog?: Abbr.
3 "Lolita" star Sue
4 Criticism
5 One with Don Juanism
6 Despotism
7 Tuna trappers
8 O-rings, e.g.
9 Rare trick taker
10 Trickery
11 Gastroenteritis cause
12 Entrapment
13 Lucifer
21 Hesitant ones
24 Man's man
25 Speed ratio
26 Mystique
27 For guys
28 Miscellany
30 With keen interest
32 Infiltrator, perhaps
34 Acceptable
35 Acquires in the end
36 "Let it stand"
40 Dons one's Sunday best
41 Occasions for holding hands
43 Not do as promised
45 Damage beyond repair
46 Plaintive piece
47 Bush-league
49 Bushman's weapon
51 "Very funny!"
52 Glamour competitor
53 "Well done!"
54 Neighbor of Minn.
55 Cravings

by Frederick T. Buhler

ACROSS

1 Opening for a coin
5 Baby buggy
9 Sell illegally, as tickets
14 Learn's partner
15 Hard to come by
16 No-no
17 Church response
18 Auction caution
19 More than plump
20 Kirstie Alley sitcom
23 Parks who wouldn't sit still for injustice
24 Ignited
25 Slangy turndown
28 On the same family tree
31 Once around the track
34 Drawings that deceive
36 Gun grp.
37 Ten: Prefix
38 New England resort
42 Very top
43 China's Chou En-___
44 "When pigs fly!"
45 ___ Moines
46 Kind of greens
49 Suffix with legal
50 Foe of the Luftwaffe: Abbr.
51 Carrot or turnip, e.g.
53 Andrew Wyeth painting
61 Sunday supper
62 Credit's opposite
63 ___ de force
64 Halo wearer
65 New York Indian
66 The "A" of Thomas A. Edison
67 Fliers in V's
68 Skyrocket
69 In case

DOWN

1 Eastern European
2 Margarita fruit
3 Walkie-talkie word
4 Pavarotti, e.g.
5 Tout
6 Mischievous one
7 "Tosca" tune
8 Clutter
9 Unemotional
10 ___ Cove ("Murder, She Wrote" setting)
11 Beame and Burrows
12 Misplace
13 Gwendolyn Brooks, e.g.
21 What's up at Rand McNally?
22 Fresh from the shower
25 Bedouin
26 Quickly
27 Bathes in sunlight
29 Smithy's device
30 Prefix with lateral or lingual
31 Bid adieu
32 Realtors' units
33 Priest
35 Hwy.
37 Recolor
39 Skyward
40 Mule on the 65-Across Canal
41 Provide with a permanent fund
46 Windsor, for one
47 Mecca's land
48 Scorecard lineup
50 Moves skyward
52 All-out
53 Rugged rock
54 Sharpen
55 Mania
56 One day in March
57 Detective Wolfe
58 Part to play
59 Brand at the bottom?
60 "Oh, fudge!"

by Gregory E. Paul

32

ACROSS

1 "Candida" playwright
5 Sings like Tormé
10 Extensive
14 Entire: Prefix
15 "La Campagne de Rome" artist
16 Aware of
17 Utah city
18 Stop on ___ (halt abruptly)
19 They can be Horatian
20 Slot machines
23 40 winks
24 Scooby-___ (cartoon dog)
25 Authorized
28 Carrier to Oslo
31 Cavaradossi's love, in opera
35 Sale items, for short
36 I.R.S. visits
38 Globe
39 Chris Evert specialty
42 ___ Bravo
43 They're in a stable environment
44 Baseball's Mel and others
45 The blahs
47 Born
48 Wall climbers
49 Org. that called 60's strikes
51 Niger-to-Libya dir.
52 Picnic event
61 Works in the garden
62 Race tracks
63 Wall Street optimist
64 Language written in Persian-Arabic letters
65 Engendered
66 Pitcher Hershiser
67 ["You don't mean . . . !"]
68 Generous helpings
69 Orangeish vegetables

DOWN

1 "Begone!"
2 Honker
3 Toward one side of a ship
4 Effeminate
5 Little rascal
6 Secret language
7 Saharan
8 Taj Mahal, e.g.
9 Lieu
10 Kind of doll
11 "The King ___"
12 Copy editor's marking
13 Chuck
21 One who blabs
22 "___ fast!" ("Hey!")
25 Unit of petrol
26 Professor Corey
27 Sing softly
28 Khartoum's land
29 Fred's light-footed sister
30 Move laterally
32 Conductor who studied under Bartók
33 Big olive oil exporter
34 Great depression
36 Farm worker?
37 Boob tubes
40 "All kidding ___ . . ."
41 Beau
46 Exhausts
48 Neither Rep. nor Dem.
50 Unkempt ones
51 Homes on high
52 Hoodlum
53 Wedding dance
54 Scarlet and crimson
55 Stuntmeister Knievel
56 Baby talk
57 Goo unit
58 New Ageish glow
59 Skelton's Kadiddlehopper
60 Additions

by Elizabeth C. Gorski

33

ACROSS
1 Nick and Nora's dog
5 Livens (up)
9 Film fragment
13 Word in an Alka-Seltzer ad
14 Alvin of dance
15 Top-notch
16 Frankie Carle's theme song
19 Teamwork deterrent
20 How some shares are purchased
21 Naugahyde coating
22 Pearl Mosque site
23 Level of karate expertise
24 Ralph McInerny novel
32 Rough-___
33 Thrill ride cry
34 "___ Believer"
35 Netman Nastase
36 Military bigwigs
38 Recite the rosary, e.g.
39 ___ Tin Tin
40 Animal shelter
41 Aunt Jemima alternative
42 Pacino drama
47 1997 U.S. Open winner
48 Went in haste
49 Bossa nova relative
52 Guardhouses
54 Lighter maker
57 Serling series
60 The Pointer Sisters' "___ Excited"
61 Like rain?
62 Clods
63 Caboose
64 Body shops?
65 Jog

DOWN
1 Cathedral area
2 Soda machine tricker
3 "___-Bungay" (Wells novel)
4 Financing abbr.
5 Cobbler container
6 Lohengrin's bride
7 House of Lords member
8 Neighbor of Isr.
9 Eyetooth
10 Advance
11 Race place
12 Orange discard
14 Elroy Jetson's dog
17 Shakespearean villain
18 Shake off
22 Queen in Dumas's "Twenty Years After"
23 Hair salon stock
24 The hot corner
25 Sun: Prefix
26 TV's J. R. or Jock
27 Tower over
28 Sounds during medical checkups
29 Sign of summer's end
30 Mature insect
31 Command to Macduff
36 Ululates
37 Narrow inlet
38 Hang fire
40 Former NBC drama
43 10-Down recipient
44 Cellulite sites
45 Skating figure
46 Observe the Sabbath
49 Swizzle
50 Words accompanied by a sigh
51 City near Phoenix
52 Sonar spot
53 Baryshnikov's birthplace
54 Wild hog
55 Dope
56 "___ la guerre!"
58 Tax court defendant, for short
59 Recurring sound effect in the comic "B.C."

by Eileen Lexau

34

ACROSS
1 Top monk
6 Indian princes
11 Come together
14 Mail deliverer's woe, maybe
15 Muse of love poetry
16 12 months, in Monterrey
17 Hanna-Barbera cartoon character
20 Encourage
21 Massages
22 "Odyssey" sorceress
23 Somewhat: Suffix
24 Roosters' mates
25 Slaves
26 Aquarium fish
28 Disfigure
29 ___ offensive (Vietnam War event)
30 Delphic utterances
34 Word before "of nails" or "of roses"
35 Agent noted for Oscar night bashes
37 School transportation
38 Son of Agamemnon
39 Needlefish
40 "___ Poetica"
41 Film units
45 Think highly of
47 Bettor's card game
50 ___ gratias (thanks to God)
51 Brief affair
52 Vogue competitor
53 Helsinki native
54 Paul Newman's role in "The Hustler"
57 Opposite WSW
58 Country west of Chad
59 Connery's successor as Bond
60 Hwys.
61 Rendezvous
62 Group belief

DOWN
1 Find not guilty
2 European stock exchange
3 Brainy
4 "___ bitten . . ."
5 Sound of disapproval
6 "Nick at Nite" staple
7 Many Mideasterners
8 1975 shark blockbuster
9 Banking convenience, for short
10 Game with a goalkeeper
11 Strangler
12 Passed, as laws
13 Bottommost
18 Rap's Dr. ___
19 Old Dodger great Hodges
24 Mata ___
25 Attacks
27 Sculls
28 ___ Diner, on "Alice"
31 Ere
32 Middles: Abbr.
33 Burning substance
34 Corner of a diamond
35 Conjectures
36 Worst possible test score
37 South Dakota geographical feature
39 Electrician on a film set
40 Silver-colored
42 Inventor of Menlo Park
43 Poe's "rare and radiant maiden"
44 Shakespearean verse
46 Abbr. on a bank statement
47 Tsetses and gnats
48 Wide-eyed
49 Game official
52 Nervously irritable
53 Sheet of ice
55 Agency head: Abbr.
56 Ambulance crew member, for short

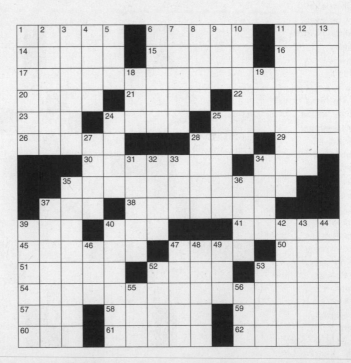

by Hugh Davis

ACROSS

1 May honorees
6 ___ A to Z
10 Notability
14 Nimble
15 ___ avis
16 Designer Cassini
17 Blakely of "A Nightmare on Elm Street"
18 Famous New York cop Eddie
19 Preceding
20 Buckle
23 Method: Abbr.
24 Sympathetic attention
25 OB/___ (certain doctor)
26 Front of a semi
29 James of "Gunsmoke"
31 Open-ceilinged rooms
33 Got 100 on, as a test
36 Expire
37 Pre-book book
38 Buckle
41 Prom queen props
42 Wonderland drink
43 Betting ratio
44 Photographer Adams
45 Window shade, e.g.
47 "Norma ___"
48 Tell a whopper
50 Part of a balance
51 Everything
54 Buckle
57 ___-in-the-bone (deeply ingrained)
60 Intravenous infusions
61 Obtain, as vengeance
62 "You ___?" (butler's question)
63 Pith
64 Small plant shoot

65 Sailor's cry
66 Model Macpherson
67 ___ voce

DOWN

1 School grades
2 It hurts
3 Part of a school grade, maybe
4 Guinness or Baldwin
5 Person who's it
6 Carte blanche
7 Spaghetti sauce brand
8 Shaggy apes
9 1975 #1 Barry Manilow hit
10 Late afternoon
11 Mountain near Zurich
12 N.Y.C. opera house, with "the"

13 Self
21 "The Blues Brothers" director John
22 Put into practice
26 Throng
27 Was laid up
28 Cotillions
29 Idolize
30 Fistfight
32 Group of Girl Scouts, e.g.
33 Essence of roses
34 Canton's country
35 Rub out
37 Underwater experiment site
39 When repeated, a Washington city
40 Spouse
45 Do a shoemaker's job
46 Word of qualification

49 Not quite grammatical answer to "Who's there?"
51 Detached
52 Legal
53 Loosen one's hold
54 Stressed out
55 Russia's ___ Mountains
56 World's fair, for short
57 Bikini top
58 "Hooray!"
59 Musician Brian

by Stephanie Spadaccini

ACROSS

1 Skiing mecca
5 Lawn eyesore
9 Donnybrook
14 Not on the rocks
15 Red Muppet
16 Chan portrayer
17 "Tell ___ the Marines!"
18 Donnybrook
19 Seeing stars
20 Start of a George Orwell quote
23 Condor condo
24 Carrier to Tel Aviv
25 Sunscreen abbr.
28 Crammer's concern
31 Time to burn
33 "___ Boot"
36 Kind of boot
38 Word with sharp or shovel
39 More of the quote
44 Gardener's pride
45 Second person
46 Night, to Nero
47 North African region
50 Wood panel feature
53 "The Racer's Edge"
54 Like most colleges
56 Cardiff citizens
60 End of the quote
64 Waikiki welcome
66 Daily delivery
67 Thunderpeal
68 Belief
69 The "I" of "The King and I"
70 Lui's partner
71 Snooker shot
72 Exigency
73 Look lasciviously

DOWN

1 Santa ___ race track
2 River in Hades
3 Devonshire dad
4 Humidor cheapie
5 "___ No Angels" (Bogart film)
6 Lamb's pseudonym
7 Chew the scenery
8 "You don't say!"
9 Fabio's forte
10 Jack of "Big Bad John"
11 Food-filled revolver
12 Hydrocarbon suffix
13 Actor Byrnes, of 50's–60's TV
21 T. follower
22 Highland refusal
26 Ragú rival
27 U.P.S. rival
29 "So that's it!"
30 Russian orbiter
32 Not worth a ___
33 ___ Ferry, N.Y.
34 G sharp's equivalent
35 Saharan stingers
37 Carry on
40 Slow throw
41 Starve
42 Hunky-dory
43 Mother, maybe
48 Former White House nickname
49 Sycophant
51 See red?
52 Old Toyota
55 Designer von Fürstenberg
57 Charles de Gaulle's birthplace
58 Like an old joke
59 Keyed up
61 "___ Gotta Have It" (Spike Lee film)
62 Supreme Court count
63 Unlike Godiva
64 24-hr. convenience
65 Grazing grounds

by Richard Hughes

ACROSS

1 Send overnight, for example
5 Hat's edge
9 Chin indentation
14 "___ girl!"
15 Deftness
16 Consumer Reports employee, e.g.
17 Hurt
18 Garage sale warning
19 Little ___ (part of the Big Apple)
20 Undergoing severe trials
23 Any of the Antilles
24 Scouting unit
25 Pharmaceutical watchdog grp.
28 Announces with fanfare
31 Lawyer: Abbr.
34 Fencing move
36 "___ dare to eat a peach?": Eliot
37 Estate division
38 Sick
42 Abound
43 Triple jump feature
44 High schoolers
45 Slalom curve
46 "25 words or less" event
49 H.S.T.'s successor
50 The "F" in F.Y.I.
51 With 7-Down, statement at a do-or-die moment
53 Ceaselessly
60 Remove dishes from
61 DeWitt Clinton's canal
62 Persia, today
63 Cooks in a caldron
64 Ancient Briton
65 Diligence
66 Pick up on
67 Easy throw
68 "What ___ can I say?"

DOWN

1 Awestruck
2 Four Corners state
3 Swizzle
4 Vietnam's capital
5 Snoopy, for one
6 Bacon serving
7 See 51-Across
8 Intertwine
9 Woody Allen's "___ and Misdemeanors"
10 Mr. Chips's class in "Goodbye, Mr. Chips"
11 Abbr. at the end of a list
12 Collapsed
13 Sample
21 Wedding worker
22 Jockey Arcaro
25 "Peter and the Wolf" bird
26 Desert features
27 Peruvian peaks
29 Skillful
30 Depressed
31 Hankered (for)
32 The way things are going
33 To the point
35 Turquoise or topaz
37 Broke bread
39 Rose feature
40 Sweetie
41 Room at the top
46 English Lit, e.g.
47 High standards
48 Bed covers
50 Mares' young
52 Bread serving
53 Burn balm
54 Bridle strap
55 Part of U.S.D.A.: Abbr.
56 Tom, Dick and Harry, e.g.
57 Mouth-to-mouth
58 Mercury and Saturn, for instance
59 On bended ___
60 "60 Minutes" network

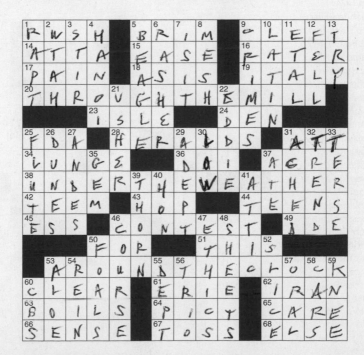

by Gregory E. Paul

ACROSS

1 Vatican City, to Rome, e.g.
8 "That's disgusting!"
11 "___ you kidding?"
14 Not as robust
15 Sib for a sis
16 Dellums or Howard
17 Discussed
19 Something to chew
20 Prefix with liter
21 Yucatán "yay!"
22 "Elder" or "Younger" Roman
23 Juliette Gordon Low, notably
27 Treaty of Nanking port
28 The Sierras, e.g.: Abbr.
29 Good buddies on the road
30 Part of a dehumidifier
31 Forbidden fruit
33 ___ Pointe, Mich.
34 Theme of this puzzle, seen seven times in the grid
36 Numbered gas rating
39 Wacko
40 Easy mark
43 French port
44 Opposite of 'tain't
45 18-wheeler
46 From Ho Chi Minh City
50 Buttonlike?
51 "___ the fields we go . . ."
52 Reached terra firma
53 W.W. II zone
54 Astonished
58 "Smoking or ___?"
59 Really cold
60 Dunk
61 Nav. rank
62 "Turn right"
63 Purse items

DOWN

1 Newt
2 Second Amendment lobby, for short
3 Where witches brew
4 Probable
5 Smart ___ (wisecrackers)
6 Of Hindu scripture
7 Victorian, for one
8 Heavy steel holders
9 Dish for Oliver Twist
10 Very popular
11 Skee-Ball and Pac-Man centers
12 Hollowing tools
13 Add one's support to
18 Lapel adornment
22 Henry ___ Lodge
23 Interstice
24 "Hallelujah, ___ Bum" (1928 hit)
25 Prefix with science
26 Tan colors
31 Beethoven's "Choral" Symphony, with "the"
32 "Intimations of Immortality," e.g.
33 Understood
34 Too big a hurry
35 Burst of wind
36 Bluer than blue
37 Caesar salad topper
38 Old Germans
40 Transparent, modern-style
41 Some radios
42 Cobbler
44 Color fabric
45 Hits, old-style
47 Alto or tenor
48 Grammy winner Judd
49 Grads
54 Rug on the noggin
55 Cambridge sch.
56 WNW's reverse
57 ___ Moines

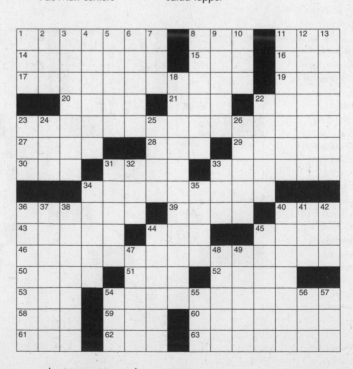

by Manny Nosowsky

ACROSS

1 Civilian clothes
6 Any Alp
10 ___ vu
14 Smiling
15 Mountain of Greek legend
16 Just-prior periods
17 E. Annie Proulx novel
20 Taoism founder Lao-___
21 Nile reptile
22 Part of MADD
23 Molded
26 Tarzan's foster mother
27 ___-Kettering Institute
29 Honeybunch
31 Kind of citizen
35 Price fixers
37 Gift label word
39 Paris-to-Amsterdam dir.
40 E. M. Forster novel
43 Kinsman: Abbr.
44 Ollie's sidekick
45 Makes things slippery
46 Former Gov. Grasso
48 Choice word
50 Gold measure
51 P.I.
53 Is here
55 Cowboy topper
59 Cry of disbelief
60 Cable's "SuperStation"
63 Jerome K. Jerome novel
66 Where to find anvils
67 Perpetually
68 Eccentric
69 Use an atomizer
70 Give stars to, perhaps
71 Provide (with)

DOWN

1 LeBlanc of "Friends"
2 Verbal pans
3 Melee
4 Woody Herman's "___ Autumn"
5 Like working plowhorses
6 Like cooked corn
7 Debatable power, for short
8 The East
9 Herbivorous hoppers
10 Turned down
11 So much as
12 Feast of Lights observers
13 Little helper?
18 Suffix with sex
19 Benetton rival
24 They may be wild
25 Arena chant
27 False alarm
28 Flap in the fashion industry
30 Dexterity
32 "I get it"
33 "Fraud" novelist Brookner
34 Minimal
36 Fashionable one?
38 Jerk's creation?
41 "For Me and My ___"
42 Spiffy
47 Bear witness
49 Run out
52 Nationality suffix
54 Actor McShane
55 Ship's front
56 Neighbor of a Laotian
57 Commits a faux pas
58 Winter Palace river
61 Capital on the Caspian
62 Ophthalmological case
64 Surfing site
65 Rock's ___ Jovi

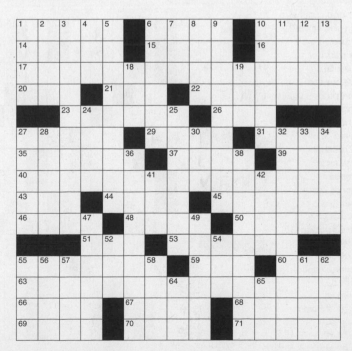

by Gayle Dean

ACROSS

1 Bird in a cornfield
5 Critters in litters
9 High-born
14 "Star Wars" princess
15 Leave out
16 N.B.A.'s Shaquille
17 Wriggling
18 Utility in Monopoly
20 Get even for
22 Tiger Beat reader
23 Tetley product
24 Gave new hands
26 A tractor pulls it
28 Tennis's Monica
30 Rise and shine
34 Grouch's look
37 Goal attempt
39 Old Italian bread
40 "Yipes!"
41 Pilot's command
42 Nincompoop
43 ". . . and ___ the twain shall meet"
44 Diatribe
45 Cast pearls before ___
46 BBQer's need
48 Home planet
50 Broad valley
52 Big-billed bird
56 Reverse of NNW
59 TV's Letterman
61 Vichyssoise ingredient
62 Fictional candy maker
65 Flour factory
66 Michael Jackson boast, in a 1987 hit
67 Ukraine's capital
68 Smell ___ (be wary)
69 Dolphins' home
70 Barely beat, with "out"
71 Barely beat, with "out"

DOWN

1 Exonerate
2 Christopher of "Superman"
3 Like smooth-running machines
4 1992 movie flop (Not!)
5 Joint Chiefs chairman during Desert Storm
6 Actress Thurman
7 Big East team
8 Exorbitant
9 "Calm down!"
10 Lennon's widow
11 Former Miss America host Parks
12 Place for a cabin
13 "Born Free" lioness
19 Do tell
21 Scotsman
25 Electrical unit named for an inventor
27 "Leaves of Grass" poet
29 1953 western
31 New Zealand bird
32 Ireland
33 "Tiny" Archibald
34 Ballad
35 One-named singer/actress
36 "You're the ___ Care For" (1930 hit)
38 Ready to draw
41 Like some undergrad studies
45 Normandy battle site
47 Celebrated bride of 1981
49 Lay down fresh tar
51 Bring to mind
53 Capital near Alexandria
54 Rand McNally book
55 Nick of "North Dallas Forty"
56 Sidestroke, e.g.
57 California's ___ Valley
58 Napoleon's home, briefly
60 Oklahoma city
63 On the ___ (fleeing)
64 Beer party staple

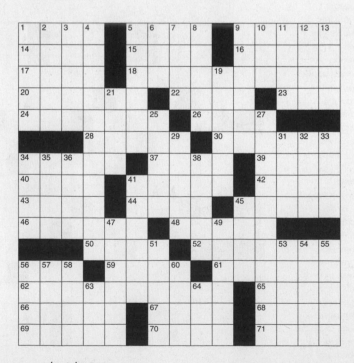

by John D. Leavy

ACROSS

1 Top Tatar
5 N.Y.C. gallery
9 Bygone A.M.C. car
14 Junction
15 Pop music's Clapton or Carmen
16 Allan-___
17 Hoary
20 Obliterates
21 "Hurry up!"
22 Scruff
23 Happy hour day, usually: Abbr.
24 "Piano," literally
26 Any doctrine
27 Eyepieces, in jargon
31 Opposite of pencil in
33 Settlement of 1624
36 Swarm
37 Give it ___ (attempt to do)
38 Wine connoisseur's concern
42 Extra life
47 Garbo, who vanted to be let alone
49 Beat the admission fee
50 Rage
51 Where Tulsa is: Abbr.
54 MSNBC competitor
55 Beats by a nose
57 Mama Cass of the Mamas and the Papas
59 Erratic move
62 Thoroughbred-breeding country
65 Sacrifice site
66 Yard pest
67 Diva Moffo
68 Steel plow maker
69 Copies
70 "Shoo!"

DOWN

1 The "K" of James K. Polk
2 19th ___ (golf clubhouse)
3 Throws in
4 Teachers' org.
5 Autobiographies
6 City near Provo
7 Pesky arachnids
8 Cause for a blessing
9 Audio systems, for short
10 Mideast's Gulf of ___
11 Channel port
12 Pass, as time
13 Shorten again, as a skirt
18 "Get outta here!"
19 Famine-stricken
23 Burn a steak on purpose?
25 ___-la-la
27 Neighbor of Que.
28 Middle grade
29 Hockey's Krupp
30 Astronomer's sighting
32 "The Joy Luck Club" writer
34 Big head
35 Propels a dinghy
39 Apt. feature, in the classifieds
40 "What ___, chopped liver?"
41 Stimpy's TV partner
43 Ear: Prefix
44 Autumn toiler
45 Concert extenders
46 Al ___ (not too soft)
47 Car's front
48 Good name
50 ___ company (running with troublemakers)
52 Andean animal
53 Journalist Stewart
56 Burn the surface of
58 Vacation spot, perhaps
59 Brass component
60 New Rochelle college
61 Pesky flier
63 Coll. senior's test
64 Kind of station

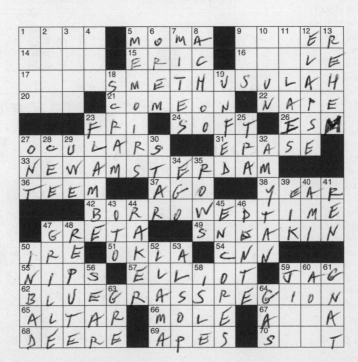

by Fred Piscop

ACROSS

1 Not for here
5 Garfield's middle name
10 Use a lot
14 No longer thinking about
15 "The Lord of the Rings" character
16 Initial, say
17 Line of collectible 1980's cards
20 Sovereign
21 Like Poe stories
22 "Fancy ___!"
23 Broadcast snafu
25 Like Samsung Corporation
28 Part of a screwdriver
29 Some newspaper pages
30 Abbreviated version
31 Diving position
35 G-man
36 Tabloid talk shows, e.g.
39 Up ___ point
40 Jockey's need
42 Sub in a tub
43 Otherwise
45 Train track
47 Grievously
48 "Oklahoma!" choreographer
51 Bash
52 In the bag
53 Astringent's target
57 Ignorers of sound diet
60 Hurler Hershiser
61 "Romola" writer
62 Lollapalooza
63 Withered
64 Taylor of "The Nanny"
65 London finales

DOWN

1 Senate attire
2 Face shape
3 Kind of warfare
4 Took a round trip?
5 Knitter's project
6 A.L. batting champ in three different decades
7 Not pouring smoothly, as a liquid
8 Org. quoted on toothpaste tubes
9 Miss Piggy, self-referentially
10 Prodded
11 Director Kurosawa
12 They form central angles
13 30's–40's bandleader Kay
18 Shocked
19 Job for a plumber
23 Hawaiian warbler
24 Use a word processor, maybe
25 Roman Catholic org. since 1882
26 Phone button
27 Start from scratch
28 Carpenter's clamps
30 "Atlantic City" director
32 The ___ Reader
33 Self-assurance
34 Stutterer's love?
37 Disturb
38 String in a string quartet
41 Sharp point
44 "In & Out" director, 1997
46 Hebrew leader
47 Show respect to
48 Karate schools
49 Accustom
50 Worker with a pick
51 Popular action figure
53 Valhalla V.I.P.
54 German article
55 Spring purchase
56 Lat., Lith. and Ukr., once
58 Anthem contraction
59 Good ___ boy

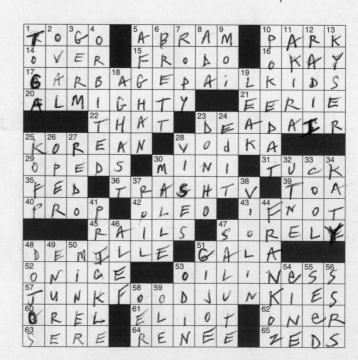

by Brendan Emmett Quigley

ACROSS

1 Borscht vegetable
5 Rip-off
9 "My dad's bigger than your dad," e.g.
14 It's all a plot!
15 Stockings
16 Raring to go
17 Gator's cousin
18 Highway
19 Sports facility
20 Cornmeal cakes, in the South
23 Piggery
24 ___ Simbel (Egyptian temple site)
25 Aardvark's diet
27 Log home
31 Brad of "Seven Years in Tibet"
33 Israeli airline
37 Orbital high point
39 Cultural grant giver, for short
40 Tick off
41 1965 Simon & Garfunkel hit, with "The"
44 Folk's Guthrie
45 Stage signal
46 One-dimensional
47 Suffix with hip or hoop
48 Another, south of the border
50 Goodman, the King of Swing
51 They may be pricked
53 Man-to-be
55 Poultry product
58 They often run deep
64 Coffee break snack
66 Bump off
67 Transport, as a load
68 Clear the chalkboard
69 Fringe
70 Capri, e.g.
71 Comparatively recent
72 Woodwind
73 Cook slowly

DOWN

1 Fugue master
2 Neutral hue
3 February 14 figure
4 "Ramblin' Wreck From Georgia ___"
5 Bush
6 Confine
7 In a hurry, for short
8 Settles disputes
9 ___ of burden
10 Boat equipment
11 Improves, as cheese
12 Telegraphed
13 Lazy Susan
21 Like windows
22 Involve
26 Unruffled
27 Spanish homes
28 To the left, to a sailor
29 Ball in the game pétanque
30 Pay no heed to
32 Deduce
34 Flax fabric
35 ___ Highway (route from Dawson Creek)
36 Suspicious
38 Accompany to a party
42 New kid in town
43 Qaddafi's land
49 Accommodate
52 September bloom
54 Had title to
55 First place
56 "Earth in the Balance" author Al
57 Chew (on)
59 Comstock, for one
60 "Now hear ___!"
61 Atlantic Coast states, with "the"
62 Be king over
63 Bunch
65 Deplete, with "up"

by Gregory E. Paul

44

ACROSS

1 White House's __ Room
5 Crafts
10 Pronto
14 Close
15 Society's 400
16 Talkative bird
17 Data
18 Alaska native
19 Yemen neighbor
20 Actress's sports award?
23 Gymnastics equipment
24 50's–60's pop vocalist __ Barry
25 Deep-space mission
28 Up to now
30 Kind of phone
33 I am, to Caesar
34 With anticipation
37 Celebrities may put them on
38 Where a TV lawyer keeps clues?
41 Cunning
42 Transylvania's locale: Var.
43 Bat wood
44 Famous Hart
45 Crow
49 Stocking shade
51 Champagne designation
53 "__ said to the . . ." (joke line)
54 Old musical producer's annual contest?
59 Reagan Secretary of State
61 Pavlov and Lendl
62 __ piece (Safire column)
63 Like a certain sax
64 Brown tone
65 Hawaii's state bird
66 Essence
67 Ore analysis
68 &&&

DOWN

1 Mystery
2 Virgil hero
3 Two-point score
4 1982 Disney movie
5 Fort __, Md.
6 Poe's middle name
7 Chicken __
8 Place for small scissors
9 6–3, 4–6, 7–6, e.g.
10 French romance
11 Formal meetings
12 Anecdotal collection
13 Greek piper
21 Place of worship
22 One NCO
26 Dueler with Hamilton
27 Spa in Germany
29 Weird: Var.
30 Studies into the wee hours
31 Movie lioness
32 City on the Rhône and Saône
35 Greek sandwich
36 Birds now raised on farms
37 Its slogan was once "Cleans like a white tornado"
38 Stance
39 Museum features
40 One of the family
41 __ Four (Beatles)
44 Actor Gibson
46 Links championship
47 Downscale
48 Marks over n's
50 Leg-of-mutton sleeve
51 Actress Braga from Brazil
52 School assignment
55 "Mona __"
56 The "Y" of Y.S.L.
57 Will Smith songs
58 __ fide
59 Hardly a beauty
60 "Aladdin" prince

Gean

E	A	S	T		M	A	K	E	S		A	S	A	P
N	E	A	R		E	L	I	T	E		M	Y	N	A
I	N	F	O		A	L	E	U	T		O	M	A	N
G	E	E	N	A	D	A	V	I	S	C	U	P		
M	A	T		L	E	N			P	R	O	B	E	
A	S	Y	E	T			C	E	L	L		S	U	O
			E	A	G	E	R	L	Y		A	I	R	S
P	E	R	R	Y	M	A	S	O	N	J	A	R		
F	O	X	Y		R	U	M	A	N	I	A			
A	S	H		M	O	S	S			E	X	U	L	T
B	E	I	G	E			S	E	C		S	O	I	
		B	I	L	L	Y	R	O	S	E	B	O	W	L
H	A	I	G		I	V	A	N	S		O	P	E	D
A	L	T	O		S	E	P	I	A		N	E	N	E
G	I	S	T		A	S	S	A	Y		A	N	D	S

by Diane C. Baldwin

me

ACROSS

1 Excuse
6 Sweetie
10 Muslim judge
14 Italian opera center
15 How draft dodgers didn't want to be classified
16 Biblical preposition
17 Seconds, of a sort
18 Husband of Ruth
19 Makes (out)
20 Start of a quip
23 Table necessity
24 "If you ___ now . . ."
25 Doctors' org.
28 King preceder
30 Life imitator
31 Union inits.
34 Quip, part 2
38 Oklahoma city
39 ___ Jima
40 Some nest eggs
41 Quip, part 3
46 West of "My Little Chickadee"
47 It often has sliding doors
48 Baseball stat.
49 Meadow
50 Rule out
51 Chemical ending
53 End of the quip
62 Show horse
63 A Ladd
64 1988 Olympics locale
65 Food found in a bed
66 Mrs. Lincoln's maiden name
67 It goes without saying
68 Longitudinal boat timber
69 Frequenters of 49-Across
70 Organic songs?

DOWN

1 Bit of Latin conjugation
2 Peru's capital
3 Holly
4 Yawn-inducing
5 As a substitute
6 Western wolf
7 Like most graffiti: Abbr.
8 A good one should be square
9 Marketplaces
10 Mission
11 "My Way" writer
12 Brain passage
13 Medicinal unit
21 Ice house: Var.
22 Grp. known for its dry comments?
25 Crosswise to a 68-Across
26 Heaven-sent food
27 Stage comment
29 Pertaining to bees
30 Battery terminal
31 Shower provider?
32 Warning fire
33 Rabies
35 Hall of "The Tonight Show"
36 Possess
37 Kind of chart
42 Bayh of Indiana
43 Require
44 ___ bien
45 Jewish festival: Var.
50 Ill-fated tower
52 Bond in a way
53 Unlit
54 Canal with a "low bridge" ("ev'rybody down!")
55 Armor-busting weapon
56 Traffic sign
57 Go in up to the ankles
58 Outcomes
59 Proper's partner
60 Folk star Redbone
61 Thanksgiving dish

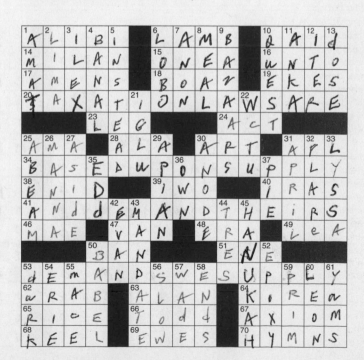

by Michael S. Maurer

ACROSS

1 Gun sound
5 Gather
10 Orioles' division, with "the"
14 Pulitzer writer James
15 Powerful camera lens
16 Early Peruvian
17 1988 Costner/Sarandon film
19 Strain at a ___
20 One in a wriggly field?
21 "I cannot tell ___"
22 Component of natural gas
24 Conks out
25 R.B.I. or E.R.A.
26 Shocked
29 Pool users
33 Unlike flat beer
34 Unnamed ones
35 Daredevil Knievel
36 Ripped
37 Baseball player news
38 Grandmother
39 Catch sight of
40 First-rate
41 NBC morning show
42 Test anew
44 Porridges
45 Christmas carol
46 Rhymer
47 Plumber's tools
50 Isinglass
51 Toledo cheer
54 Either end of a magnet
55 1984 Redford film
58 Lotion ingredient
59 Platform part, perhaps
60 Cincinnati nine
61 Entre ___ (confidentially)

62 Brewer's need
63 Protuberance

DOWN

1 George Herman Ruth, familiarly
2 Malaria symptom
3 Little Dickens girl
4 It keeps hair in place
5 Charm
6 "61 in '61" slugger Roger
7 Throb
8 Mrs., in Madrid
9 Occasional
10 1988 Cusack film
11 The "I" of "The King and I"
12 Scrutinize
13 London art gallery

18 "She loves me, she loves me not" flower
23 ___-o'-shanter
24 1958 Hunter/Verdon film
25 Stockholm resident
26 Subsequently
27 Barnyard honker
28 Heavenly strings
29 1953 western hero
30 Circumvent
31 Of the kidneys
32 Does in
34 One way to fish
37 Wall hanging that tells a story
41 Pick up the tab
43 Broadway's "Five Guys Named ___"

44 Junior's jalopy?
46 Yearns (for)
47 Bridge
48 ___ contendere
49 Baseball's Matty or Moises
50 Tableland
51 Cookie favorite
52 29-Down player
53 Otherwise
56 Shake a leg
57 Ornamental vase

by Kenneth Witte

ACROSS

1 Andy's pal
5 Decent-sized diamond
10 Latin I word
14 Term of endearment
15 Kitchen appliance brand
16 Shed
17 LIGHTS!
20 Chop down
21 Actress McClurg
22 DNA structure
23 Carolina college
24 Bradley, the G.I.'s General
26 Composer Gustav
29 Moot
33 Red as ___
34 ___ Cove, L.I.
35 Cotton gin maker Whitney
36 CAMERA!
40 Troupes for the troops: Abbr.
41 Appearance
42 Bisect
43 Traitorous
46 Joke that causes a belly laugh
47 Franchise
48 "Stop waiting around!"
49 Heart pitapat
52 Animation frames
53 Average guy
56 ACTION!
60 French cleric
61 Fishing craft
62 One conquered by Pizarro
63 Unfairly deprives (of)
64 Playful animal
65 Big bovines

DOWN

1 1970's hitmakers from Sweden
2 "Manifesto" writer
3 Bassoon's cousin
4 The Bering, e.g.
5 Where Duncan was done in
6 Forcefully
7 Widemouthed Martha
8 "What else?"
9 ___ chi ch'uan
10 Unit named for a French physicist
11 "___ Flanders"
12 Jai ___
13 Crossing for Charon
18 Computer order
19 Spawning fish
23 Ht.
24 Indian, e.g.
25 "Death in Venice" author
26 Conductor Kurt
27 Mistreat
28 "Great blue" bird
29 French avenue
30 Board
31 "As ___ and breathe!"
32 Fall drink
34 Dance move
37 "___ my wit's end"
38 ___ longue
39 Bridge seat
44 Calls forth
45 Asian expanse
46 Woods, e.g., or one who uses woods
48 11-Down's creator
49 Stowe lift
50 Tracks traveler
51 L.B.J. in-law
52 Serial abbr.
53 Foredoom to failure
54 Fairy tale opener
55 Actor Richard
57 Earth-friendly prefix
58 Used a 38-Down
59 Carnival site

by Randy Sowell

scar

dafoe ME
defoe MIEN

48

ACROSS

1 Sporty Mazda
6 Name for a colleen
10 Actor Johnny
14 Tannenbaum topper
15 "Tell ___ lies"
16 Lamb alias
17 1981 drama starring Treat Williams
20 D.C. dignitary
21 Prelim
22 Slip cover?
23 "___ jolly swagman . . ." ("Waltzing Matilda" start)
24 Soul, in Soissons
25 Spenser opus
32 It's right in the atlas
33 It may be proper
34 Frequent Powell co-star
35 Dalloway or Doubtfire
36 XXX drink, in the comics
39 Singing the blues
40 ___ Lilly and Co.
41 Princess tormentor
42 Kind of dancer
44 Arabian Sea nation
45 Tennyson's 12-poem series
50 Shoebox letters
51 Isn't insensitive
52 "Bulletproof" actor Henry
55 Photographer Cartier-Bresson
56 Scheming
59 Expressionistic O'Neill play
62 A driver may change one
63 Goatish glance

64 Get out of bed
65 Bookie's quote
66 Auto pioneer
67 Overexcited

DOWN

1 They may provide relief
2 Apropos of
3 Opposed to, in Dogpatch
4 Rare gymnastics score
5 Handel opera
6 Ham
7 Chorus
8 Gung-ho about
9 Japanese drama
10 Authoritative order
11 Writer Wiesel
12 Orchestra areas
13 Is beneficial
18 Suffix with differ
19 Onetime Secretary of State Muskie
23 Frequently, poetically
24 Blue hue
25 Adagio and allegro
26 Ran fast, in England
27 16-Across work
28 Aurora's Greek counterpart
29 Varnish resin
30 Pitcher Ryan
31 Gawking at
36 Radiant
37 Meet one's Waterloo
38 Narcissist's problem
43 Bid
44 Endorses

46 Some banks
47 Barbershop quartet members
48 Munich Mr.
49 Mendelssohn oratorio
52 Normandy battle site
53 "___ no idea!"
54 Play the pawnbroker
55 Bread end
56 Use shears
57 ___-majesté
58 River of Flanders
60 Arafat's grp., once
61 "Kid" of jazz

by Nancy S. Ross

ogleam
gleaming

ACROSS

1 Check
5 Fill to excess
9 Country bumpkin
13 New Jersey city
14 All-night teen parties
16 Send off
17 DIAMOND
20 Lilliputian
21 Ready to serve
22 They're trouble for roses
23 Bass, for one
24 ___ Fox
25 SQUARE
33 Honeydew, e.g.
34 Spa
35 Excessively
36 Parched
37 Bug
38 One of Columbus's ships
39 Words at the altar
40 Senator John
41 Like a shoe
42 CIRCLE
45 Peaches
46 Idiom: Abbr.
47 Sound choice
50 Look
52 1936 candidate Landon
55 TRIANGLE
58 Sounds from Hawaii
59 Legend in automotives
60 Top spot
61 Meal eaten in a hall
62 They get in the way of sound thinking
63 More than lean

DOWN

1 Great deal
2 Character
3 Lip
4 "Mamma ___!"
5 Dishes with syrup
6 Hardly believable
7 Pizza place
8 Money for a Toyota, say
9 One of the Beverly Hillbillies
10 Mine, in Marseille
11 Species
12 Alpine off-seasons
15 Stiff
18 ___ Heights
19 Viewfinders?
23 Give ___ to (approve)
24 Relay sticks
25 Screen letters
26 "Rigoletto" composer
27 "The Hollow Men" poet
28 Doubleday and others
29 Fran Drescher TV role
30 Beneficial
31 Fair-sized musical group
32 Parasite
37 Colorado city on the Rio Grande
38 Film genre
40 Actress Garson
41 Jerk
43 Way out
44 Works by 26-Down
47 Pigsty
48 Puff
49 Party times
50 Complacent
51 River in Spain
52 Purina competitor
53 Mortgage
54 Good-lookin'
56 Secure, as a victory
57 Prattle

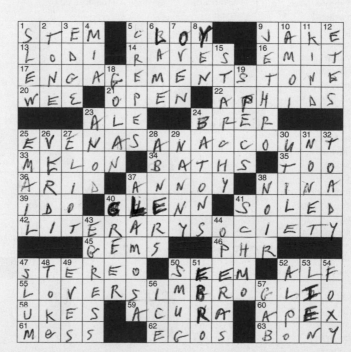

by Alan Arbesfeld

MCAIN
McCain

ACROSS

1 Major no-no
6 Fruity pastry
10 Superdeluxe
14 Primitive weapon
15 Brainstorm
16 Have the throne
17 Rural dance
18 Like a seven-footer
19 They give people big heads
20 Fast-paced card game
23 Having three unequal sides, as a triangle
26 Act like aloe
27 SOS lights
28 Use an ax
29 German auto
30 Austen novel made into a 1996 movie
33 Most-wanted group of attendees
38 Wear one's best
41 Cosmetician Lauder
42 Ewes' calls
43 Chase Manhattan, e.g.
44 Proofs of age, for short
46 Dictation takers
48 Esoteric
52 Kleptomaniac
54 Gymnasts' quests
56 Banned apple spray
57 Pitcher Hershiser
58 Dueler's sword
63 Roman philosopher
64 "__ M for Murder"
65 Like some piano keys
66 Larry King has a few
67 Award for Oprah
68 Renter's paper

DOWN

1 Sugar amt.
2 Part of a milit. address
3 Actress Barbara __ Geddes
4 Acorn, eventually
5 Seer
6 Mythical giant
7 In __ (befuddled)
8 Count (on)
9 "Thy Neighbor's Wife" author
10 Ragú competitor
11 Should, with "to"
12 Animal that sleeps upside-down
13 Literature Nobelist Hermann
21 Bowler's button
22 Des Moines native
23 "Yellow-bellied coward" and others
24 West Point drillee
25 Stand up
27 Lose color
28 More than a tee-hee
31 Sale scenes
32 N.Y.C. subway manager
34 Newspaper no-no
35 Nonsensical
36 Man of La Mancha
37 Head-shakers' syllables
39 Paris bisector
40 German industrial city
45 Read, as enemy messages
47 Mortarboard part
48 With speed
49 "Take it easy"
50 Egg protector
51 60's–70's coifs
52 Fulton's power
53 What to watch the BBC on
55 Quick haircut
59 Pres. Lincoln
60 Showy scarf
61 Ems followers
62 Seedy loaf

by Elizabeth C. Gorski

ACROSS

1 Check
5 Fill to excess
9 Country bumpkin
13 Pretentious
14 Deposed leader's fate, maybe
16 Chester Arthur's middle name
17 DIAMOND
20 Airport info, informally
21 On the safe side, at sea
22 Math groups
23 Here, to Henri
24 Calcutta clothing
25 SQUARE
33 Klingon or Vulcan
34 Women's group?
35 Coach Parseghian
36 Buster Brown's dog
37 Central points
38 First governor of Alaska
39 Loser to R.M.N. in '68
40 Numbers game
41 Sharp
42 CIRCLE
45 One who's on your side
46 London lav
47 Bother
50 In a frenzy
52 Take a part
55 TRIANGLE
58 Lago contents
59 Seasonal visitor
60 Efficient
61 Actress Schneider
62 Hoot
63 Not a hit or an out

DOWN

1 "Streamers" playwright David
2 Part of Q.E.D.
3 Frank Capra's "___ Wonderful Life"
4 Bill ___, the Science Guy
5 Protect, as freshness
6 Bridge toll unit
7 Floor unit
8 Actor Wallach
9 Kind of bread
10 1997 Peter Fonda title role
11 Latvian, e.g.
12 Volumes A and Z in an encyclopedia
15 Boxes
18 Part of a hearty breakfast
19 Discussion medium
23 "Mm-hmm!"
24 Somewhat
25 Prefix with logical
26 Peace Nobelist Root
27 "Oh, sure"
28 Yankee Hall-of-Famer Ford
29 Must
30 International court site, with "The"
31 Plenty sore
32 Jury
37 Atheistic
38 Return to the Alps?
40 French textile city
41 Came to
43 Square dance move
44 Baseball's Roberto
47 Frost
48 Jason's ship
49 Refuse
50 "Rule, Britannia" composer
51 "G'day" recipient
52 Palindromic pop group
53 It makes a bit of a stir
54 Hard journey
56 ___ Mahal
57 Stomach

by Alan Arbesfeld

ACROSS

1 Stormed
6 Narc bust
10 Lab container
14 A bouquet has one
15 Fairy tale beginning
16 As regards
17 Intransigent senator's tactic
19 "Miss ___ Regrets" (1934 hit)
20 Ivan or Nicholas
21 "The Catcher in the ___"
22 Johnnie Cochran entreaties
23 Taste and touch
25 1996 award for "The English Patient"
27 Dull
31 Farm units
35 Adjutant
36 Egyptian fertility goddess
38 Show muscle?
39 Had a role to play
40 "Laura" director Preminger
41 Tennille of the Captain and Tennille
42 Mail delivery paths: Abbr.
43 Photographer Adams
44 Survive inspection
47 Death row reprieves
48 Gives way
53 Two-___ (deceitful)
55 "The Gold Bug" writer
57 Undecorated
58 "You said it, brother!"
59 Rural flier
62 Healthful mineral
63 "Take this!"
64 Building modification
65 Villa d'___
66 Land west of Nod
67 Calendario opener

DOWN

1 Whitewater transports
2 Get out of bed
3 ___ Heights (disputed Mideast area)
4 Kuwaiti rulers
5 Bit of ointment
6 Optimistic
7 Opening wager
8 Diamonds, in criminal slang
9 "___ Rosenkavalier"
10 Reason for a ticket
11 Hobbies
12 Pavarotti solo
13 Minus
18 Constellation bear
22 Compaqs, e.g.
24 Chicago trains
25 "The ___ trick in the book!"
26 Engaged in litigation
28 Saguaro
29 Toys with tails
30 Baptism, for one
31 Not fore
32 Hoof sound
33 Making a comeback
34 Being
37 The sun
39 Team from West Point
43 "Exodus" hero
45 In low spirits
46 Examined
49 Buddy of 60's–70's TV
50 Motorized shop tool
51 Bleak, in verse
52 ___-Croatian
53 Disconcert
54 "Lucky Jim" author
55 Read (over)
56 Many a tournament
59 Cuban hero Guevara
60 Like sunsets
61 Yorkshire river

by Randall J. Hartman

ACROSS

1 Hemmed, but didn't haw
6 Israel's Dayan
11 Tout's offering
14 Tickle pink
15 Expressed joy
16 The self-proclaimed "Greatest"
17 Trifling amount
19 Singer Zadora
20 10% cuts
21 ___ fields (mythological afterworld)
23 Spot for a Band-Aid
26 Take apart
27 School zone sign
31 Pirate's potable
32 Korean soldier
34 New Zealander
35 Black cat, maybe
37 Stallone role
41 Dorothy followed it
44 Seaweed-wrapped fare
45 Rights org.
46 Agnew's plea, for short
47 New Haven collegian
49 Racket or rocket add-on
50 Breslau's river
51 Scold, with "out"
54 Scottish "sighting"
57 Cracker shapes
59 Bring to light
64 Ancient lang.
65 "Coal Miner's Daughter" actress
68 Order to attack, with "on"
69 Cynic's look
70 "Dallas" matriarch
71 Volcanic spew
72 They're pitched at jamborees
73 Is cockeyed

DOWN

1 The Amish, e.g.
2 K–12, scholastically speaking
3 Restaurant annoyance
4 Produce art on copper, e.g.
5 Rink fakeouts
6 Presidents' Day, e.g.: Abbr.
7 Punch-in-the-stomach reaction
8 Followers
9 Ward ___ (local politico)
10 Water whirled
11 Gimme on the green
12 Trojan War epic
13 "Eighty-eight"
18 Third-party account
22 Indonesia's first president
24 Cuban dance
25 Slaps a fine on
27 "The ___ the limit!"
28 Place
29 Temple footballers
30 Knuckleballer Hoyt
33 Sitcom planet
36 Frasier's TV brother
38 General feeling
39 Hoedown seat
40 Wavy lines, in the comics
42 Fix a squeak
43 Radioactivity units
48 Kind of skates
51 Glider wood
52 Diarist Nin
53 Broom Hilda, e.g.
55 Krupp works city
56 Boot out
58 Helper: Abbr.
60 Robust
61 Pac 10 sch.
62 "Deal ___!"
63 ___ out (manages)
66 Ready
67 Jr. and sr.

by Fred Piscop

54

ACROSS

1 Kind of shower
7 Bedroom furniture
14 Treat with gas
15 "Gunsmoke" deputy
16 Mythical warrior
17 Consolidated clockmaker?
19 Give off
21 Teachers' org.
22 Cleopatra biter
23 Oldenburg "oh!"
26 Private reply, maybe
28 Oktoberfest supply
29 Valerie Harper TV role
32 Start of many ship names
33 "Peter Pan" heroine
34 Consolidated composer?
37 Decree
38 Popular radio format
42 Consolidated singer?
46 Wistful exclamation
49 Stir
50 Accepted rule
51 Actor's goal
52 Office folk
54 Literary monogram
55 Yalie
56 Ally of the Fox tribe
57 Kismet
60 Consolidated puzzle author?
63 Mountainous
67 Distinguished
68 Headline-making weather phenomenon
69 Deviation
70 Places to sit, paradoxically

DOWN

1 Cry to Bo-peep
2 "Losing My Religion" rock group
3 Brother of 34-Across
4 Stun
5 Focus for Fermi
6 Red Square figure
7 Heat beaters: Abbr.
8 Like Cologne and environs
9 Taxi feature
10 Workplace regulator, for short
11 "What was ___ think?"
12 Stay
13 Eliminated, in a way
18 Like a little old lady in tennis shoes?
20 Hit the road
23 Ship on which Heracles sailed
24 "Moonstruck" star
25 Cascades mount
27 Induction grp.
28 Former aerospace giant
30 Adorned, in a way
31 Light-footed
33 Mrs. Flintstone
35 Alfonso XIII's queen
36 Court
39 Brief O.K.: Abbr.
40 They can be bruised
41 Between 0% and 100%
43 Jeer
44 Cretan peak
45 Remove
46 Couturier Cassini
47 Mother of Constantine the Great
48 Get closer to, in a race
52 Brazilian dance
53 Passengers
56 Dog-paddled, e.g.
58 Conclusion of some games
59 Poet ___ St. Vincent Millay
61 Ike's W.W. II command
62 Marshal under Napoleon
64 Conclusion of some games
65 Conclusion
66 Bits of advice

by Gene Newman

ACROSS

1 Diminished over time, as the moon
6 Model T starter
11 15-Across swung one
14 French novelist Zola
15 Baseball's Hammerin' Hank
16 Grow old
17 "Great" words from Jerry Lee Lewis
19 Sought office
20 Tallow source
21 Like a haunted house
23 Cosmetics
27 Name to a position
29 Not these or those
30 Artist Eric
31 Time on the job
32 Physical stature
33 Letter after pi
36 Tennis units
37 Gnatlike insect
38 St. Paul's architect Sir Christopher
39 Before, in poetry
40 Alternative to a convertible
41 Appearances
42 Lustrous cotton fabric
44 Harsh
45 Clothes with slogans
47 Charity event
48 Second City's #1 airport
49 Weapon swung by a gaucho
50 Needlefish
51 "Great" Asian landmark
58 Indiana Jones's quest
59 "The Waste Land" poet
60 Word after dog or jug
61 Bro's sibling
62 "You Light Up My Life" singer Boone
63 Drive too fast

DOWN

1 Spider's snare
2 Doctors' grp.
3 Nothing
4 Building wing
5 Tapioca pudding, e.g.
6 Parisian diners
7 Huck Finn's conveyance
8 Jackie's second
9 "___ any drop to drink": Coleridge
10 Patella protector
11 "Great" Australian landmark
12 Once more
13 Group belief
18 Mine and yours
22 Seemingly forever
23 Sheriff's group
24 Weasel relative
25 "Great" ocean predators
26 TV rooms
27 True up
28 True north spot
30 Khartoum is its capital
32 Waits
34 Artist Matisse
35 Beginning
37 Make the acquaintance of
38 Marry a woman
40 Scattered, as seeds
41 What Dennis does to Mr. Wilson
43 Lungful
44 The individual
45 Ceremonial gowns
46 Puppeteer Lewis
47 Ill-gotten gains
49 Splotch
52 Pub choice
53 Women's ___
54 See by chance, with "upon"
55 Intense anger
56 Maiden name preceder
57 Use an abacus

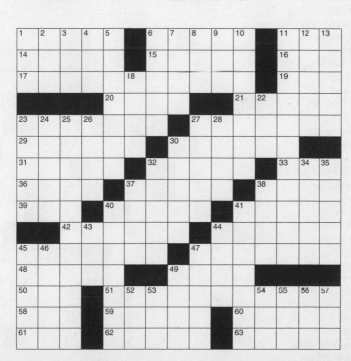

by Mark Moldowsky

ACROSS

1 "You are here" posting
4 Hawkeye Pierce portrayer
8 Result
14 Sign that all are welcome
16 Floodgate
17 Like a swift and spectacular success
18 Do a slow burn
19 Fabled thieves in green
21 "The ___ Mutiny"
23 H.S. math
24 Sounds of hesitation
25 California fort named for a Union general
26 Circumspect
30 Fill to the ___
32 Small-business magazine
33 Asimov and Newton
37 Civil rights activist Parks
38 It'll make you red in the face
40 Mallorca, e.g.
41 Spinning
43 Black gunk
44 Wash cycle
45 Augusta golf tourney
47 CPR expert
48 Ecol. watchdog
51 First person in Berlin
52 Where to get Seoul food
54 Ivy League rooters in green
59 Taking the place (of)
60 Face decoration for a brave
63 "You ___ bother!"

64 Person-to-person
65 They can be liquid or frozen
66 Distort
67 Actor Beatty

DOWN

1 Tattoo word, often
2 King Kong
3 Culture container
4 Desert clay
5 Actress Singer of "Footloose"
6 "___ What Comes Natur'lly" (Irving Berlin song)
7 Flatfoot's lack
8 Fighters in green
9 Sorority candidates
10 Takes to court
11 Words to a blackjack dealer

12 Yellow pigment
13 Many MTV watchers
15 It's a gas
20 Row your boat
21 Charmer's snake
22 Cupid's dart
26 Cookie sellers in green
27 Popular card game
28 Sharp as a tack
29 Speaker's spot
31 Hurt badly
34 Slanderous insinuation
35 General weather conditions
36 Holiday visitor
39 Civil War grp.
42 Clothing
46 Turkey day: Abbr.

48 Patsy's pal on "Absolutely Fabulous"
49 Window pieces
50 Site in a Bizet suite
52 Sound of a punch
53 "Chestnuts roasting ___ open fire"
55 Ocean motion
56 Ark groupings
57 Bit of hair
58 At no cost
61 Opposite SSW
62 Cable kingpin Turner

by Nancy Salomon and Bob Klahn

ACROSS

1 Under ___ (concealed)
6 Woman's shoe
10 "Cease and desist!"
14 Irene, Dike and Eunomia
15 Positive
16 Stigma
17 Spooky board
18 Kind of list
19 ___ Beauty (apple variety)
20 "Finally!"
22 Food
24 Honest one
25 ___ & Chandon (champagne)
27 Diamond middleman?
29 Herb sometimes called Chinese parsley
33 For example
34 Computer type
35 Writer Jaffe
37 Fixed tire
41 ___ foo yung
42 Coroner's concern
44 "Eureka!"
45 Frothy
48 Way of speaking
49 Formal hat, informally
50 Lawyer's hurdle
52 Frightening
54 First-rate
58 Korean statesman
59 ___ Tomé and Príncipe
60 College sports org.
62 Disgust
66 Polo competitor
68 Summit
70 Bellyache
71 Nimble
72 Football's Armstrong
73 Later
74 Hinders legally
75 Corset prop
76 Cooped up at Old MacDonald's

DOWN

1 "Hold it!"
2 Beat badly
3 Seed covering
4 Bit of bedwear
5 Rainy or silly follower
6 Camera setting
7 Pear-shaped instrument
8 Spheres
9 Tithe amounts
10 Abbr. on old Asian maps
11 Paint job finale
12 Pentameter parts
13 Questionable cradle location
21 Aquarium fish
23 Glide aloft
26 "Speckled" fish
28 Bread for a Reuben
29 G ___
30 Betrayer of the Moor
31 Women's Tour sponsor: Abbr.
32 Fully informed about
36 Ed of "Lou Grant"
38 Mob boss
39 Doubt-conveying interjection
40 Peel
43 Refrain in many early Beatles songs
46 Entrepreneur's deg.
47 Gape
49 Hush-hush
51 Right-hand pages
53 Rules
54 Up on deck
55 Stuns
56 Locale for Santa's team
57 Singer Bonnie
61 Samoan capital
63 Fuzzy fruit
64 Sporting rapier
65 Bookworm
67 Toper's woe
69 Stowe girl

by Susan Smith

58

ACROSS

1 "___ Howdy Doody time!"
4 Bit of gravel
9 "Falstaff" or "Fidelio"
14 Singer ___ King Cole
15 Lecture hall platforms
16 Boxcars, in dice
17 Barbecue dish
19 Open, as a bottle
20 Weird
21 "Cómo ___ usted?"
23 Enlivens, with "up"
24 Developments
26 One "E" on a scoreboard
28 Street urchin
32 Nay canceler
35 Load for Jack and Jill
36 Madcap
38 9-Across solo
40 Fairy tale figure
43 Bird on a beach
44 Malden and Marx
46 Scores 72 on a 72 course
48 Lair
49 Kind of timing
53 Slowdown
54 Deep Throat, e.g., in the Watergate scandal
58 Kill, as a dragon
60 Not slack
63 Smells
64 Birchbark
66 Nolan Ryan specialty
68 Bread spreads
69 Pale purple
70 NNW's opposite
71 Hornets' cousins
72 Very, very thin
73 Word before "more" and "merrier"

DOWN

1 Map within a map
2 Become narrower
3 Gawk (at)
4 Acceleration
5 Craggy peak
6 Garfield's canine pal
7 Bird beaks
8 It ends Lent
9 The Buckeyes: Abbr.
10 Locate exactly
11 Quoted (from)
12 Sow's opposite
13 Nile snakes
18 Bathtub detritus
22 Horace's "___ Poetica"
25 Without women
27 Genetic initials
29 Kind of foil
30 Skip the usual wedding preparations
31 Land of the leprechauns
32 Tibetan ox
33 Paleozoic and Mesozoic
34 Hangar contents
37 Larry King employer
39 Cartoon caveman
41 Rock's Fleetwood ___
42 Son of Aphrodite
45 Take a chair
47 Pub game
50 Egyptian boy king
51 Muscle tics
52 Surfer's sobriquet
55 Barnyard perch
56 Puppy love
57 Cosmetician Lauder
58 Flat-bottomed boat
59 Singer's refrain
61 Beehive State
62 Loyal
65 Super G curve, in the Olympics
67 "___ Got a Secret"

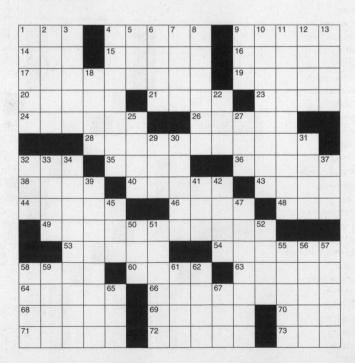

by Randall J. Hartman

ACROSS

1 Remote control button
5 Secure a ship
9 Hunter's trail
14 Pinnacle
15 Poet Pound
16 Mare : foal :: cow : ___
17 Sicilian spouter
18 Arabian Sea adjoiner
19 Hit the + key
20 Mrs. Morgenstern player on "Rhoda"
23 Watchdog's warning
24 Japanese dog
25 Explorer who named Louisiana
27 ___ Plaines, Ill.
28 Barnes & Noble habitué
32 Hi's helpmate, in the comics
33 Witchy woman
34 Buenos ___
35 Marxist exiled by Stalin
38 ___ Valley, Calif.
40 Out of dreamland
41 Saws
42 Cafe or cabaret
44 Pompous sort
47 Listened to again, as legal arguments
49 16 drams
51 Unusual shoe width
52 "Guys and Dolls" writer
56 Visit the registrar
58 Concept
59 Dairy airs?
60 Screen star Keaton
61 Wander
62 Poker pot starter
63 Man of La Mancha
64 Pulls a boner
65 "Untouchable" Eliot

DOWN

1 Attendant on Dionysus
2 Slow on the ___ (thickheaded)
3 With 44-Down, court query
4 Obtain by demand
5 Siamese sound
6 Baum princess
7 Kind of exam or history
8 Irritate
9 Surgical souvenirs
10 Hippie's hangout
11 The Stars and Stripes
12 Be situated atop
13 Set right
21 Peter of Peter, Paul & Mary
22 Pitcher part
26 Comparable
29 Long, long time
30 Cupboard crawler
31 Rid of vermin
33 Put an end to
34 "Now I ___!"
35 Like most Danish churchgoers
36 Have bills
37 Old salt
38 Lengthy discourses
39 Hattie McDaniel's "Show Boat" role
42 The Roaring Twenties, e.g.
43 Look up to
44 See 3-Down
45 Moves along quickly
46 Taste and touch, for two
48 Freud contemporary
50 Deprive of one's nerve
53 Scent
54 Approach
55 Namath's last team
57 Lennon's widow

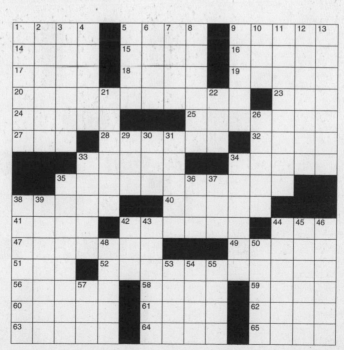

by Patrick Jordan

ACROSS

1 King Tut's favorite card game?
5 Bilko and York: Abbr.
9 Moola
14 Visa rival
15 Cow's flyswatter
16 Split, old-style
17 Gimlet garnish
18 As to
19 ___-ski
20 "St. John the Baptist" painter
23 "Come again?"
24 Outlaw
25 "Six Characters in Search of an Author" dramatist
34 Dole out
35 Toast topper
36 River islet
37 Pac 10 team
38 Rising star
40 Stimulate
41 "The Crying Game" star
42 Collagist's need
43 "Ditto"
44 NBC Symphony conductor, 1937–54
48 Basilica bench
49 Winner of 10/30/74
50 "Norma" composer
59 "What ___!"
60 Director Kazan
61 Bumped off
62 Thornburgh's predecessor as Attorney General
63 Sound off
64 Long skirt
65 Where to find favors
66 People
67 Not fooled by

DOWN

1 Take a spill
2 Friend of François
3 San ___, Italy
4 The yoke's on them
5 Rouse
6 Best Picture of 1982
7 Novice: Var.
8 Take to the hills?
9 Swagger
10 Complain
11 Be a breadwinner
12 Tours with?
13 Lucie's dad
21 Make ___ with (please)
22 Daisy Mae's mate
25 Gene Tierney title role
26 Tummy trouble
27 ___ ease
28 ___ few rounds
29 Shakespearean eloper
30 Stout relative
31 "Funny About Love" star Christine
32 Use, as a cot
33 10th-century Holy Roman emperor
38 Make faces, say
39 Like Ellen, now
40 Cyst
42 New York Tribune founder
43 Camelot coat
45 Tossed skyward
46 Texas-Louisiana border river
47 Traction enhancers
50 Theda Bara, e.g.
51 Think tank product
52 ___-do-well
53 Round number
54 "The Good Earth" heroine
55 Car with a bar
56 Self-confident words
57 Cry to the queue
58 Peculiar: Prefix

by Bette Sue Cohen

ACROSS
1 Reply to a ques.
4 Wisecrack
8 Youngster
13 Brag about
15 Wrist-elbow connector
16 Cowboy contest
17 Defeats
19 Traveler's reference
20 Composer who wrote "The Magic Flute"
21 "Don't go out!"
23 Speaker's spot
25 Medicinal herb
26 Become motionless out of fear
30 Pass, as time
34 Thin fish
35 "This ___" (shipping label)
37 Unprepared comment
38 Actor Guinness
40 Plants used to make poi
42 Without: Fr.
43 Discipline
45 Popular athletic footwear
47 Golf bag item
48 Baroque and rococo, e.g.
50 Opposite of 26-Across?
52 Apollo astronaut Slayton
54 Suffix with gang
55 Unwanted art
59 Fanatic
63 U. S. Grant opponent
64 Opposite of 17-Across?
66 Deduce
67 Gloomy
68 Bubbly beverage
69 Castles' barriers
70 TV deputy from Hazzard
71 Armenia or Azerbaijan, once: Abbr.

DOWN
1 Tiny particle
2 Porto-___ (Benin's capital)
3 Canal that leads to the Red Sea
4 Division result
5 German city on the Danube
6 Chemical endings
7 Macaroni and such
8 Colorful brand name?
9 Rash people
10 Not busy
11 Shakespearean king
12 Prescription amount
14 Barter
18 Mania
22 Bubbly beverage
24 Land south of Egypt
26 Is afraid of
27 On again, as a lantern
28 Poem of lament
29 Jewish festival
31 Philosopher who wrote the "Republic"
32 Tendon
33 Actor Buddy
36 Nudges
39 Opposite of 9-Down?
41 Bubbly beverages
44 Illegal cigarettes, slangily
46 Turn the wheel
49 Do slaloms
51 Pulls
53 Conservatory assignment, perhaps
55 Bleak
56 Clinton Attorney General
57 ___ Romeo (Italian auto)
58 Let ___ a secret
60 Facilities, in Falmouth
61 Multivolume ref. works
62 Pre-1917 ruler
65 Twosome

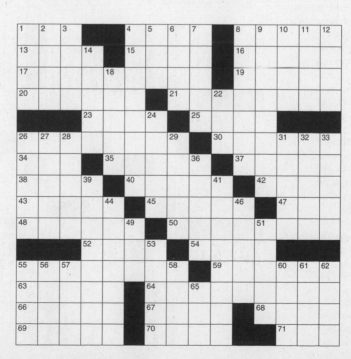

by Jeremy Thomas Paine

62

ACROSS

1 Religious scroll
6 Coat, as with plaster
10 Group with the 1976 hit "Fernando"
14 Solo
15 Fare for Fido
16 Medicinal weight
17 Domingo, for one
18 Smack
19 Indian music
20 1991 best seller by Jim Stewart
23 It laps the shore
26 Trump's "art"
27 ___ de Cologne
28 "___ soul man" (Blues Brothers lyric)
29 Trains on high
31 Circumference
33 Sheepish response
34 Neighbor of Mex.
37 Lowbrow sitcom staple
41 Bro's counterpart
42 Lend a hand
43 Nattering type
45 Scandalous 80's initials
46 "___ Compères" (1984 film)
48 Suffix with Sudan
49 Hon
53 All over the place, as paint
56 Secret diet-breakers
58 Western Indians
59 Lévesque of Québec
60 Out-and-out
64 Elder, for one
65 Midmonth date
66 Info-packed
67 Pronounces
68 "Hey, you!"
69 American-born princess

DOWN

1 Work on a doily
2 ___ Miss
3 Director Howard
4 Where to connect one end of a jumper cable
5 Enclosed, in legalese
6 Noted Big Apple residence, with "the"
7 "Get ___!"
8 Against the current
9 Hooey
10 See eye to eye
11 Accolade for Von Stade
12 Deli item
13 Accumulate
21 Site of 60's tour of duty
22 Bouncers check them: Abbr.
23 Parlor drink
24 Poetic feet
25 Mideast emirate
30 "Well, ___-di-dah!"
32 The "I" of T.G.I.F.
33 Ogler's target
34 Actress Thurman
35 Clearheaded
36 Left one's seat
38 Lab runner
39 Sesame paste source
40 Discomposed
44 Rest stop?
45 Nuptial starter
46 Most recent
47 Season in Bordeaux
49 Aberdeen folk
50 Extremist
51 Like hot fudge
52 Dolts
54 Glazier's items
55 Fragrant compound
57 Stumble
61 J.F.K. terminal
62 Computer key, for short
63 Popular toast

by Elizabeth C. Gorski

ACROSS

1 Do a double take, e.g.
6 Affluence
11 It paves the way
14 Result
15 Four-time N.L. home run leader
16 Till bill
17 Finishing touch
19 Dos Passos trilogy
20 Pope's " ___ Solitude"
21 Taken around the track
23 Winded
26 How the tabloids tell many stories
27 Consolidates
28 Pacific
29 "Your place or mine?" and others
30 Hormone regulator
31 Dupe
34 End piece
35 Jeweler's glass
36 Pickle
37 Hydrocarbon suffix
38 KFC leavings
39 Linen fabric
40 Fishing nets
42 Justice from New Hampshire
43 Tough puzzle, informally
45 Own
46 Prove it!
47 German-born Surrealist
48 Azimuth
49 Terrorist's alias
54 Toothpaste type
55 Public relations concern
56 "The American Crisis" pamphleteer
57 She-sheep
58 Pleiades number
59 Tea drinker's request

DOWN

1 Kind of room
2 Rock's Brian
3 Tempe inst.
4 Preference
5 Collectible stuffed toys
6 Son of Japheth, in Genesis
7 Merit
8 Football's Parseghian
9 Feature of Mendelssohn's "A Midsummer Night's Dream"
10 Wore a belittling look
11 Right now
12 Photographer Adams
13 Alert
18 Twilights, poetically
22 Avarice, e.g.
23 Actor Tom
24 Kind of jack
25 Circa 1895–1900
26 Vaults
28 Swings around
30 Hopeless case
32 Van Gogh locale
33 Jury members
35 Wanting company
36 Aqualung inventor
38 Some beachwear
39 50-50 situations
41 Rank on "Star Trek": Abbr.
42 Something to break into
43 Phase
44 Lost on purpose
45 Get gussied up
47 Keenness
50 Dallas cager, for short
51 Outfit
52 Genetic initials
53 Always, in poems

by Jonathan Schmalzbach

64

ACROSS

1 "Dear old" guy
4 Where Nome is
10 Nick and Nora's pooch
14 N.Y.C.'s ___ of the Americas
15 ___ to go
16 Urban haze
17 Tiny bite
18 Pat
20 Pet
22 ET's craft
23 Patriot Allen
24 Ozs. and ozs.
26 Facial spasm
29 Lucy's hubby
30 Kid's reply to a taunt
33 Cousin of "Oy!"
34 Della of "Touched by an Angel"
36 Suave actor David and others
38 Pit
40 Virginal
42 Unclouded
43 Sentry's "Stop!"
44 Europe's "boot"
46 Hounds
50 Yale student
51 ___ glance
52 Jazzman Blake
53 Spoil
55 Pot
59 Put
62 Chinese leader Sun ___-sen
63 "___ That a Shame" (#1 hit for 18-Across)
64 Scottish children
65 Opposite of WSW
66 Methods
67 Refuse to yield
68 Decimal point

DOWN

1 Tangoed, e.g.
2 Fly a plane
3 Ocean bottoms
4 Fire-setting crime
5 Lion's home
6 Florence's river
7 Ink a contract
8 Prepares to pray
9 Farming: Abbr.
10 Beginning on
11 Not so bumpy
12 Coal delivery unit
13 Grow older
19 City transit
21 Most equitable
25 Billy the Kid's surname
27 Country restaurant
28 Fortune 500 listings: Abbr.
30 Falseness
31 Common language suffix
32 Bing Crosby's record label
33 Add extra music to, as a vocal tape
35 Chow down
37 "Give ___ rest!"
38 Ex's payment, modern-style
39 Right-angled bend
40 Guerrilla Guevara
41 Falstaff's prince
45 Alternative to Maytag or KitchenAid
47 Followed orders
48 Jeans brand
49 Six-line poem
51 Biblical boat
52 ___ & Young (accounting firm)
54 Play parts
56 Elevator innovator
57 Opera's ___ Te Kanawa
58 Geologic periods
59 Observed
60 Spanish aunt
61 Japanese sash

by Mark Danna

ACROSS

1 What jazz ends with, in England
5 Leaves in, editorially
10 One who's decamped?
14 Linen color
15 George Eastman's company
16 1996 Campaign name
17 With 39-Across, often-quoted work of 1923
20 Sot
21 Oval
22 Campus mil. org.
25 90 degrees, on a compass
26 Unit of oil production: Abbr.
29 Matter to go to court over
31 Linen colors
35 Statement from Pinocchio
36 Old-fashioned music hall
38 River to the English Channel
39 See 17-Across
43 Evil one
44 Common dice roll
45 Expected
46 Single-celled organisms
49 Austin-based computer company
50 Knight
51 More than a snack
53 Stir up
55 Tropical woe
58 Israeli native
62 What 17- and 39-Across is
65 Rainbows
66 Rips to pieces

67 Saroyan's "My Name is ___"
68 TV sleuth Fletcher, to friends
69 Wear away
70 Abysmal test score

DOWN

1 Part of an orange
2 Prefix with plasm
3 Tiniest bit
4 Marvelous
5 Schuss, e.g.
6 Quite a load
7 Advantage
8 Coffee ___
9 1973 NASA launch
10 Alternative to pregnancy
11 Coaxes
12 Kind of shoppe
13 "___ Miz"

18 Subatomic particle
19 Judicious
23 List heading
24 Ship's handlers
26 Rarity for a century plant
27 "That's it!"
28 Absorb facts
30 Played (with)
32 Diagrams
33 Ho-hum feeling
34 Rocker Bob
37 "Well, I ___!"
40 Like some stockings
41 Prefix with -drome
42 Sign up
47 Expensive
48 "Les Mouches" dramatist
52 One with no hope of getting out
54 Capital of Bolivia

55 Extra
56 The basics
57 Cartoonist Peter
59 Reduce to tears, maybe
60 Stern
61 BB's and such
62 The Brits in colonial India
63 Unusual
64 Atlanta-to-Tampa dir.

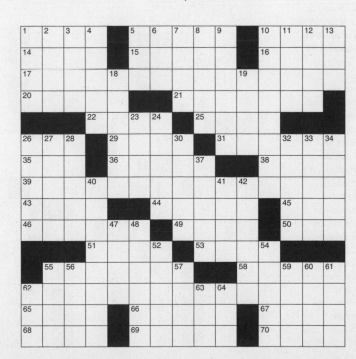

by Bill Ballard

66

ACROSS

1 Start of many instructions
6 Important Phoenician city
11 Letters from 12-Down
14 Carlo Levi's "Christ Stopped at ___"
15 Penned
16 80's White House nickname
17 Month after Adar
18 Keep an ___ the ground
19 Literary olio
20 Emergency food of Operation Overlord?
22 Pup's cry
23 Overjoys
24 They may have a crush on you
25 College conferrals
28 "___ she blows!"
30 They may be slippery
31 Taboo
36 ___ mode
37 Michael Caine spy movie
39 Tuck's partner
40 Writer's joy
42 Downyflake alternative
43 Kind of flea or dollar
44 Astronomical phenomenon
47 Wallet wad
49 Magna ___
51 CD-___
52 Chalet support, possibly
57 Pan Am rival
58 Sugarcoat
59 With 63-Across, comics girlfriend
60 "Bali ___"
61 Worn away

62 Zaragoza sir
63 See 59-Across
64 Resided
65 Paradises

DOWN

1 Ward (off)
2 Kin of op. cit.
3 Parks of civil rights
4 Hit men
5 Crystal chandelier sound
6 Endures apprehensively
7 More than miffed
8 Day of "Pillow Talk"
9 Director Preminger
10 Broadway blinker
11 Do a post-Challenger diagnosis

12 Ancient Greek colony
13 Loses control
21 "Norma ___"
24 "Kapow!"
25 Refusing to listen
26 Actress Raines
27 F.B.I. agent's communication
28 Mom's offering
29 Hasten
32 Emolument
33 Heavens
34 Andrews of "The Mod Squad"
35 "Fix"
37 TV's Matlock
38 Inc., overseas
41 Vegas opener
42 Licensed
45 Sourdough's find
46 Of no use
47 Straight: Prefix

48 "Nothing doing!"
49 Jalopy
50 Eye color
52 Like sharp cheese
53 It may be fatal
54 One from Hanover
55 "Lucid" stream, to Thomas Gray
56 Sartre's seas

by Robert H. Wolfe

ACROSS

1 From a distance
5 Zeal
10 Wrestling surfaces
14 Writer Ephron
15 Chessman
16 Here, in Honduras
17 ___ Alexander (Hall-of-Fame pitcher)
20 Surgery tool
21 Zsa Zsa's sister
22 Slander's counterpart
23 CBS logo
24 It makes the heart grow fonder
27 Is for more than one?
28 Middle of a simile
29 Last number in a countdown
31 ___ Duke (tobacco magnate)
38 Police officers
39 Yankee manager Joe
40 Common dog's name
42 Dadaist Jean
43 ___ non grata
45 Also
46 ___ Yello (soft drink)
48 Snooze
49 Gown
51 "The magic word"
53 Portuguese islands
54 ___ Toole (Pulitzer-winning novelist)
58 Tiff
60 Golfer's gouge
61 Corp. bigwig
64 Circle parts
65 Best of a group
66 Requirement
67 Stopped sleeping
68 Meted (out)
69 Sounds of disapproval

DOWN

1 What a protractor measures
2 Quick raid
3 Got out of bed
4 Great review
5 Busy mo. for the I.R.S.
6 Reduces to bits, as potatoes
7 Search (into)
8 Pacific, for one
9 Gun the engine
10 Niger's western neighbor
11 Gulf between Saudi Arabia and Egypt
12 Piano fixer
13 Move furtively
18 Clear the chalkboard
19 Actress Verdugo
25 Moisten the turkey
26 Former Maine Sen. William
28 Mornings, for short
30 Naval rank: Abbr.
31 Superman's father
32 Fermented cider
33 Brought to life
34 ___ Major (Great Bear)
35 Riding whip
36 Kiwis
37 Gallows loop
38 Pitch a tent
41 Light throw
43 Fancy-schmancy
44 Axlike tool
47 Noted Chinese philosopher
50 Mouse or beaver, e.g.
52 Finished
53 Chipped in chips
55 Amount in a drug shipment
56 Wicked
57 Memo
58 Trite saying
59 In favor of
62 Mouse hater's cry
63 Record store purchases

by Peter Gordon

68

ACROSS

1 Site of St. Peter's
5 Leg muscles, for short
10 Swindle
14 "Jeopardy!" host Trebek
15 Reversed
16 Former California Gov. Wilson
17 Itsy-bitsy skirt
18 Precalculator calculators
19 Corrida cheers
20 "Dallas" ranch
22 Fountain servings
23 Union letters
24 Airline seating class
26 Matzohs lack it
30 Early screen star Power
32 Axis foes
34 At any time, in poetry
35 Physics units
39 Teen hangout
40 50's bandleader Perez ___
42 Cross inscription
43 East European
44 ___ Lingus
45 Samples
47 Off the mark
50 A century after the Wright brothers' first flight
51 Like an old oak tree
54 G.I. entertainers
56 Cinema chain
57 Diving maneuver
63 First name in gymnastics
64 City south of Bartlesville
65 Point after deuce, maybe
66 ___ dire (legal process)
67 Have ___ of tea
68 Karate school
69 Start of North Carolina's motto
70 Catapult missile
71 Muhammad and others

DOWN

1 St. Louis 11
2 Hodgepodge
3 Carte
4 Kind of poll
5 Hearty draft
6 Open, as a barn door
7 Month after Shebat
8 Haggled
9 Star Wars, initially
10 "Hoobert Heever," e.g.
11 Rostropovich's instrument
12 Mr. T's TV show, with "The"
13 Cluttered
21 Bigot's emotion
22 Swindle
25 French landscape painter
26 Thanksgiving bowlful
27 Mideast carrier
28 ___ breve (2/2 time)
29 Theme of this puzzle
31 Pine
33 Alley score
36 Part of ABM
37 Three of a Kind?
38 Asunción assent
41 Adapt anew
46 One way to run
48 19th-century literary inits.
49 Arizona territorial capital
51 Fielder's aid
52 Legal pleas, informally
53 Umbrella
55 Play for the N.H.L.
58 Gravy Train competitor
59 Zippo
60 Pop star
61 South Seas getaway
62 Genesis son
64 Univ. instructors

by Mark Elliot Skolsky

ACROSS

1 Commercial creator
6 Bor-r-ring
10 Coal carrier
14 Uninviting to a vegan
15 Composer Schifrin
16 Kind of mechanic
17 Saying of Benjamin Franklin, part 1
20 Red, to a motorist
21 Big ___ house
22 Oktoberfest mementos
23 Bunyan's tool
24 Fuel gas
25 Like some pay rates
29 Chimney channel
30 Indian state
31 One who does the lord's work
32 Tag info
36 Saying, part 2
39 One-named Nigerian singer
40 Smooth-talking
41 Homologous
42 Heirs, often
43 They feature Franklin
44 Quoting the raven?
47 Calendar square
48 In a breezy way
49 Polish off
50 Novelist Haley
54 End of the saying
57 More than one way to skin ___
58 "Well, ___ that special!"
59 Encircle
60 Just say no
61 "One-l lama" poet
62 Florida citrus center

DOWN

1 "Lucky Jim" author
2 Nimble
3 It may be held in delis
4 Resting on
5 Big Apple sch.
6 World-weary
7 Superboy's girlfriend
8 Cover girl Carol
9 Sexy one, in slang
10 "___ hike!"
11 Quarrel
12 Observe Yom Kippur
13 Cuts (down)
18 Like candles
19 Will-wisp connection
23 Soprano Gluck
24 N.F.L. Hall-of-Famer Hirsch
25 Boater and sailor
26 Org. concerned with working conditions
27 Preowned
28 Pan's opposite
29 Has a hunch
31 Plaintiff's action
32 Recital performance
33 Monogram part: Abbr.
34 Quarterback Bratkowski
35 Spuds' buds
37 Bughouse
38 More than a few
42 Rural sight
43 Either of two Roman statesmen
44 "Odyssey" enchantress
45 Indo-European
46 Like Oscar Wilde
47 Vader of "Star Wars"
48 Slightly
49 Fish-eating birds
50 "Hold on ___!"
51 ___ Linda, Calif.
52 Biographer Ludwig
53 "Warrior Princess" of TV
55 Spanish she-bear
56 Reporter's question

by Thomas W. Schier

ACROSS

1 Labyrinth
5 Murders, mob-style
9 Numbers on baseball cards
14 ___ Brothers of 40's–50's music
15 Pink, as a steak
16 Sign in an apartment window
17 Head honcho
19 Think out loud
20 Michaelmas daisy
21 Prefix with metric
22 Like most sumo wrestlers
23 Kind of preview
25 Carpenter's machine
26 Droop
29 Roadhouse
30 Nuisance
31 More smooth
33 Medieval weapons
37 Lima's land
38 Relatives of the English horn
40 Pharaohs' river
41 Shivered
43 Persians, today
45 Slippery
46 "___ Mir Bist Du Schoen" (1938 hit)
47 Bombast
48 Gets the 7–10 split
51 Sheriff's symbol
53 Gypsy's deck
54 Have title to
55 Beginning
59 "Don't tell ___!"
60 Head honcho
62 "What ___ to do?"
63 Presently
64 Tickle-me doll

65 Tapes sent to recording companies
66 Classic political cartoonist
67 Card game start

DOWN

1 Doll's cry
2 Writer Kingsley
3 Piquancy
4 Adlai's 1956 running mate
5 Bobby of the Bruins
6 One-named 50's–60's teen idol
7 Search, as for weapons
8 Kind of lily
9 Informer
10 Head honcho
11 Nonnational
12 Uptight
13 One of the cattle in a cattle drive
18 Actor Kovacs
24 Signs up
25 Shaky
26 Mo. when Libra starts
27 Swear
28 Richard of "Primal Fear"
30 "Rue Morgue" writer
32 Head honcho
33 Pea container
34 Ped ___ (traffic caution)
35 Director Kazan
36 Meeting: Abbr.
39 Old Turkish pooh-bah
42 June bugs, e.g.
44 Severity
46 Folk music instruments
48 Conservative
49 Out of style
50 "___ With a View"
51 Master, in Swahili
52 Closed
54 Neighbor of Yemen
56 Shoe bottom
57 Jane Austen novel
58 Hammer or sickle
61 Toronto's prov.

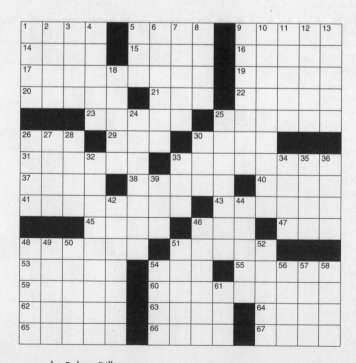

by Robert Dillman

ACROSS

1 Pilgrimage to Mecca
5 Weather vane turner
9 It may have its own registry
14 Lamb's pen name
15 Champagne bucket
16 Pep ___
17 Catalogue abbr.
18 Twins player in "Big Business"
20 Gathered, as berries
22 Spinks of the ring
23 Suffix with Japan or journal
24 French father
26 Bronx cheer
28 Models of excellence
32 "The Crimes of Love" author Marquis ___
36 List-shortening abbr.
37 Recital piece
39 Betray, in a way
40 Terhune's "___ Dog"
41 Upright
43 Region
44 Lively Highland dance
46 Parcel (out)
47 Aspersion
48 Pizza portions
50 City on San Francisco Bay
52 Coup d'___
54 Late Chinese leader
55 Attorneys' org.
58 Soprano's song, maybe
60 Get ready
64 Twins player in "Start the Revolution Without Me"

67 Skeleton part
68 Part of UHF
69 Pound of poetry
70 Skip over
71 Shelley's "Adonais," e.g.
72 Tailor's meeting place
73 Assign an "R," say

DOWN

1 Rope fiber
2 Et ___ (and others)
3 Kind of jockey
4 Twins player in "House of Numbers"
5 Sweetbrier
6 Here, to Héloïse
7 "The Old Curiosity Shop" girl
8 Clothesline alternative
9 Get-tan-quick application
10 Zodiac animal
11 Supermodel Macpherson
12 Ivy League team
13 Bit of force
19 Warty hopper
21 Brain-wave test, briefly
25 Vast, in the past
27 Twins player in "The Girl in the Kremlin"
28 Ill-gotten gains
29 To any extent
30 Wheel spokes, e.g.
31 Catch some Z's
33 Ring around a lagoon
34 Cruller's cousin

35 January, in Jalisco
38 Group of eight
42 Pre-fax communiqué
45 Vacation spot
49 Rani's wrap
51 A wee hour
53 Scrabble pieces
55 Chills and fever
56 Dinger
57 Chip in chips
59 Axlike tool
61 "Arrivederci ___"
62 Condo division
63 Tennis's Sampras
65 Bit of work
66 Time to remember

by John Greenman

ACROSS

1 Arctic dwellers
6 Vegetate
10 Irving protagonist
14 Belief of 1.1 billion
15 Thompson of "Sense and Sensibility"
16 "Essays of ___," 1823
17 It's tucked under the chin
18 Farmer's prayer, perhaps
19 1994 Jodie Foster film
20 Valentine present?
23 Parisian parent
24 Motorists' org.
25 Piedmont wine center
28 Passionate
31 Not to mention
34 Grassy plain
36 1953 Pulitzer playwright
37 "Turandot" slave
38 Valentine present?
42 Pithecanthropus relative
43 Fare
44 Iota
45 Composer Rorem
46 On-the-job learner
49 Fish, to herons
50 Lineman
51 Monique's eye
53 Valentine present!
60 Delete
61 Overly bookish sort
62 Pharmacy solutions
64 Naysaying
65 Just the ___
66 Prom dress material
67 50+ percent

68 Substitute for the unnamed
69 Certain fisherman

DOWN

1 Year Claudius died
2 The East
3 Trudge
4 Popular parade horse
5 Urban air pollution
6 "Gigi" lyricist
7 Five-star Bradley
8 Gallic girlfriend
9 Spanish dance
10 Setting for Verdi's "Simon Boccanegra"
11 Pub quaffs
12 Nettle
13 Comrades
21 Pitching stat.

22 Honey badgers
25 Berg of "Lulu" fame
26 Incline
27 Burdened
29 Electron tube
30 Abbr. at the bottom of a letter
31 Modify
32 Agnes, to Cecil B.
33 Somewhat dark
35 In the ___ (likely to happen)
39 Abridge
40 Tap word
41 Sewn-on cutout design
47 Short poem on two rhymes
48 Bottom line
50 Suffer a humiliating loss, in slang

52 Breathing fire
53 Course finale
54 Talking during a film, e.g.
55 Fortitude
56 Crux
57 Humorist Bombeck
58 Nonexistent
59 Severe blow
63 Homily: Abbr.

by Nancy S. Ross

ACROSS

1 Cleopatra's love ___ Antony
5 Scrabble play
9 Cosmetician Lauder
14 On the briny
15 Verdi's "D'amor sull'ali rosee," e.g.
16 Con man
17 List component
18 Datum
19 Bronco catcher
20 Good-time Charlie
23 Norway's capital
24 Embarrassing sound, maybe
25 Mouse catcher
28 Airedale, for one
31 Volcanic fallout
34 Playing marble
36 Building wing
37 Forearm bone
38 Best
42 Mishmash
43 Coach Parseghian
44 Kingdom
45 Fishing gear
46 Chicago newspaper
49 "Treasure Island" monogram
50 Wilt
51 Use Western Union, e.g.
53 Noble one
60 Diamond weight
61 Bit of thatching
62 Like hen's teeth
63 Martini garnish
64 ___ Spencer, brother of Princess Diana
65 Stadium section
66 Passover meal
67 "If all ___ fails . . ."
68 Child's Christmas gift

DOWN

1 Pony Express load
2 ___ spumante
3 Coral ridge
4 Alfred Hitchcock film appearance, e.g.
5 Breakfast dish made on an iron
6 Patrick Henry, for one
7 Rolling in dough
8 Whom one goes out with
9 Cream-filled pastry
10 Astute
11 Dry run
12 "No problem"
13 Ike's W.W. II command
21 Bone: Prefix
22 Suave competitor
25 Dinner rooster
26 Like a gymnast
27 Implied
29 Recovery clinic
30 Suffix with percent
31 Where "I do's" are exchanged
32 Tackle box item
33 Injures
35 Ring result, briefly
37 Indian with a sun dance
39 North Dakota's largest city
40 The first "T" of TNT
41 "Goodnight" girl of song
46 Make ragged
47 Wedding workers
48 Pine leaf
50 Spartacus, e.g.
52 Pub game
53 December 26 event
54 Rainless
55 At no cost
56 Dabbling duck
57 Banister
58 Arbor Day honoree
59 Group of cattle
60 Comedian Bill, to friends

by Gregory E. Paul

ACROSS

1 Irene of "Fame"
5 B.A. and B.S., e.g.
9 Try to avoid a tag
14 Throat clearer
15 Eye amorously
16 Kitchen counter?
17 1996 Clinton challenger
18 Stand in line
19 More slippery
20 How to succeed as a stripper?
23 Opposite WNW
24 Letterman's network
25 Heir's concern
28 Vandalize
30 Start with down and out
32 Fourposter, e.g.
33 Stops
35 Areas between hills
37 How to succeed as a retailer?
40 Voting districts
41 Go light (on)
42 Getting on in years
43 Govt. book balancers
44 Lucky plant
48 Puts in office
51 "Tsk!"
52 First lady
53 How to succeed as a demolition crew?
57 Fine dinnerware
58 Ready and willing's partner
60 Finito
61 "Prizzi's ___"
62 Hit alternative
63 Just in case
64 They're cutting, sometimes
65 Sports figure?
66 Greek god of love

DOWN

1 Bummed
2 What Richard III offered "my kingdom" for
3 Load off the mind
4 "You can say that again!"
5 Somewhat pessimistic
6 "Yikes!"
7 Smooth-talking
8 ___ good example
9 Mudholes
10 On the up and up
11 Worthy of copying
12 "Look at Me, I'm Sandra ___"
13 Miscalculate
21 Means of approach
22 One of Lee's men
26 Ball props
27 Asner and Begley
29 Kind of test or rain
30 Addict's program
31 Takes advantage of
34 Flower supporter
35 Jumps with a pole
36 Brand for Bowser
37 Room connector
38 Bossing
39 Most safe
40 Grief
43 Sugar suffix
45 Presidential nixer
46 Nonetheless
47 Racks the pins again
49 Trapper transport
50 Russian autocrats: Var.
51 Oklahoma city
54 Thanksgiving potatoes
55 Passing notice
56 In neutral
57 ___ Guevara
58 Coal carrier

by Nancy Salomon

ACROSS

1 Dash competitor
4 Fraction of a joule
7 Pertaining to city planning
14 Writer LeShan
15 6-Down formation
16 City of southern Italy
17 Kind of pistol
18 Genesis name
19 Crow, for one
20 Tommy Moe's specialty
23 Lose strength
24 "Bad Behavior" star Stephen
25 Old Broadway star Ruby
29 Go down
31 First U.S. color-TV maker
33 Rhoda's mother on "Rhoda"
34 Out-of-date
37 Pop group with the #1 hit "End of the Road"
40 Venezuelan river
42 Animal with a herd mentality
43 Slum life documentarist
45 Stooge
46 Have chits out
47 They: Fr.
48 Cause of Chinese restaurant syndrome
49 Seuss character
52 "___ Ran the Zoo"
54 Overhang
58 Khomeini was one
61 Add a coat
64 Half a colon
65 You can dig it
66 Three-horse carriages
67 Dream Team letters
68 Blade
69 In a nasty way
70 Tuba note?
71 Zipper cover

DOWN

1 Joltless joe
2 Morris or Stewart of Arizona
3 Rocker Frank
4 Flush
5 Studio effect
6 Canada ___
7 Hollywood's Morales
8 Suicidal
9 Actress Graff
10 Twilled worsted
11 Prefix with lateral
12 Place to turn in
13 How some packages arrive
21 "___ kick from champagne . . ."
22 Syrup brand
26 55 or 65, perhaps
27 Heavenly abodes
28 Long-limbed
30 "We're not supplying liquor"
32 V-8's eight: Abbr.
34 Objects carrying magic spells
35 Suburb of Tokyo
36 Command to Fido
37 Swelter
38 Devilkins
39 They're sometimes spitting
41 Felon
44 Does the chasing in tag
48 Brunch drink
50 "Let me repeat"
51 "Take ___!" ("Get lost!")
53 Sick and tired
55 Standoffish
56 Like the flu
57 Nail smoother
59 Minuscule
60 Four Corners state
61 Some linemen: Abbr.
62 West ender?
63 Starchy dish

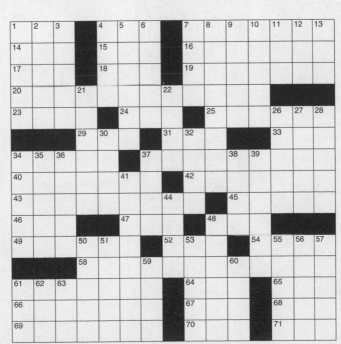

by Fred Piscop

The New York Times

CROSSWORDS

PUZZLES FOR ALL OCCASIONS

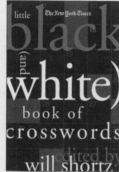

Available at your local bookstore or online at nytimes.com/nytstore.

St. Martin's Griffin

1

```
S I L A S   ■   S A T   ■   ■   L U S H
A T A L L   ■   P S I   ■   R E N T E
C A C T I   ■   A H A   ■   E N D E R
S L E E P E R   ■   R E L O O P S
■   ■   R U Y   ■   D A D A   ■   ■
E R A   ■   P E T E   ■   S I N N E D
P A C T   ■   O I L S   ■   D E U C E
O V E R   ■   F L I P S   ■   I D L E
D E R E K   ■   E V I E   ■   L E A D
E L B E R T   ■   E T N A   ■   S T S
■   ■   A V E R   ■   A N S   ■   ■
G A T E M A N   ■   S T I N K E R
I N A W E   ■   A D O   ■   M A N G O
G O N E R   ■   C O D   ■   A R E A S
I N K S   ■   ■   T W A   ■   L E E D S
```

2

```
M A R C   ■   D O G M A   ■   M A L T
A R I A   ■   A C R E S   ■   A L O E
W E L L   ■   M E A N S   ■   R A G E
■   A L I E N A B D U C T I O N
■   E V E N   ■   M R I   ■   ■
V E I N E D   ■   O R I E N T A L
I N S T   ■   S T A N D   ■   A V A
C E L E B R I T Y G O S S I P
A R A   ■   O O Z E S   ■   A S A P
R O M A N C E R   ■   L E M O N S
■   ■   K K K   ■   S A M S   ■   ■
E L V I S S I G H T I N G S
L O O M   ■   T O R A H   ■   E L A L
B U L B   ■   A L O N E   ■   A U N T
A S T O   ■   R A W E R   ■   D E E D
```

3

```
P O M P   ■   D A D A   ■   R A D A R
A M I R   ■   I B I S   ■   U V U L A
I N R I   ■   L E A S   ■   B A C O N
L I O N H E A R T E D   ■   K E G
■   T A M M Y   ■   C O I F   ■
N A P A L M   ■   R O W B O A T
A L I D   ■   A S T O   ■   N O O S E
R A G   ■   A S P E C T S   ■   T O X
C R E A M   ■   A L S O   ■   L E N A
S M O K E R S   ■   M A I D E N
■   N A T E   ■   S T O M A   ■
A L T   ■   H A R E B R A I N E D
R O O M Y   ■   I G O R   ■   S I L O
A L E C S   ■   M A N O   ■   O L I N
M A D A T   ■   S L E W   ■   N E A T
```

4

```
A B H O R   ■   S E G A   ■   S O L E
B L A R E   ■   C R O W   ■   I N O N
B E L E T T E R P E R F E C T
R U S S I A N S   ■   A T T A R
■   ■   E X T   ■   U S S   ■   O L E
M A M A S   ■   S P A S   ■   ■
O B I S   ■   S C H E L L   ■   R A J
P U S H T H E E N V E L O P E
S T S   ■   I O D I D E   ■   O D E S
■   P E E K   ■   Q U E S T   ■
U N I   ■   T D S   ■   T A U   ■   ■
P I N T O   ■   H O R I Z O N S
S T A M P O F A P P R O V A L
E R N E   ■   W I N S   ■   E L E V E
T E E N   ■   E G G Y   ■   D A R E D
```

5

```
E S T O P S   ■   P R O M   ■   O D D
R A H R A H   ■   O O N A   ■   V I A
S H O R T E N E D S T R E E T
E L M   ■   C R I M E   ■   A O R T A
■   ■   P A R T   ■   F D A   ■   ■
P A R I S I A N P R O N O U N
S L A S H   ■   A J A R   ■   C H I
Y O D A   ■   G A S S Y   ■   S C U T
C H A   ■   O L L A   ■   C O U R T
H A R M F U L L I G H T R A Y
■   ■   A F T   ■   B A A S   ■   ■
A S P I C   ■   W H E L P   ■   S R O
G E R M A N A U T O M A K E R
E V A   ■   S O N G   ■   R A V I N E
D E Y   ■   T R E E   ■   E N A M E L
```

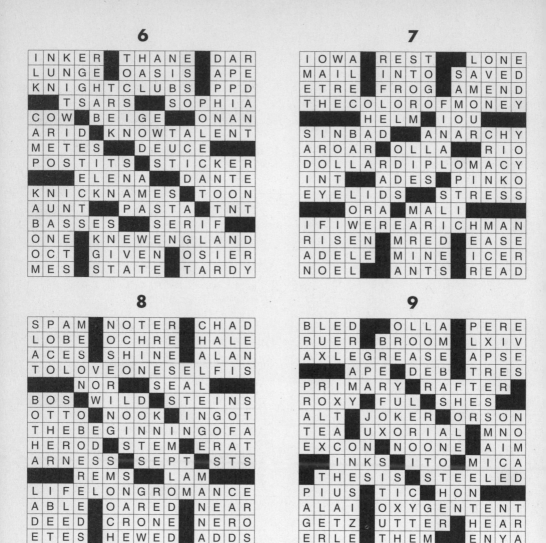

6

```
I N K E R ▪ T H A N E ▪ D A R
L U N G E ▪ O A S I S ▪ A P E
K N I G H T C L U B S ▪ P P D
▪ ▪ T S A R S ▪ ▪ S O P H I A
C O W ▪ B E I G E ▪ ▪ O N A N
A R I D ▪ K N O W T A L E N T
M E T E S ▪ ▪ D E U C E ▪ ▪
P O S T I T S ▪ S T I C K E R
▪ ▪ E L E N A ▪ ▪ D A N T E
K N I C K N A M E S ▪ T O O N
A U N T ▪ P A S T A ▪ T N T
B A S S E S ▪ ▪ S E R I F ▪
O N E ▪ K N E W E N G L A N D
O C T ▪ G I V E N ▪ O S I E R
M E S ▪ S T A T E ▪ T A R D Y
```

7

```
I O W A ▪ R E S T ▪ ▪ L O N E
M A I L ▪ I N T O ▪ S A V E D
E T R E ▪ F R O G ▪ A M E N D
T H E C O L O R O F M O N E Y
▪ ▪ ▪ ▪ H E L M ▪ I O U ▪ ▪
S I N B A D ▪ A N A R C H Y
A R O A R ▪ O L L A ▪ ▪ R I O
D O L L A R D I P L O M A C Y
I N T ▪ ▪ A D E S ▪ P I N K O
E Y E L I D S ▪ ▪ S T R E S S
▪ ▪ ▪ O R A ▪ M A L I ▪ ▪
I F I W E R E A R I C H M A N
R I S E N ▪ M R E D ▪ E A S E
A D E L E ▪ M I N E ▪ I C E R
N O E L ▪ ▪ A N T S ▪ R E A D
```

8

```
S P A M ▪ N O T E R ▪ C H A D
L O B E ▪ O C H R E ▪ H A L E
A C E S ▪ S H I N E ▪ A L A N
T O L O V E O N E S E L F I S
▪ ▪ N O R ▪ S E A L ▪ ▪ ▪
B O S ▪ W I L D ▪ S T E I N S
O T T O ▪ N O O K ▪ I N G O T
T H E B E G I N N I N G O F A
H E R O D ▪ S T E M ▪ E R A T
A R N E S S ▪ S E P T ▪ S T S
▪ ▪ R E M S ▪ L A M ▪ ▪
L I F E L O N G R O M A N C E
A B L E ▪ O A R E D ▪ N E A R
D E E D ▪ C R O N E ▪ N E R O
E T E S ▪ H E W E D ▪ A D D S
```

9

```
B L E D ▪ ▪ O L L A ▪ P E R E
R U E R ▪ B R O O M ▪ L X I V
A X L E G R E A S E ▪ A P S E
▪ ▪ A P E ▪ D E B ▪ T R E S
P R I M A R Y ▪ R A F T E R ▪
R O X Y ▪ F U L ▪ S H E S ▪
A L T ▪ J O K E R ▪ O R S O N
T E A ▪ U X O R I A L ▪ M N O
E X C O N ▪ N O O N E ▪ A I M
▪ ▪ I N K S ▪ I T O ▪ M I C A
▪ T H E S I S ▪ S T E E L E D
P I U S ▪ T I C ▪ H O N ▪ ▪
A L A I ▪ O X Y G E N T E N T
G E T Z ▪ U T T E R ▪ H E A R
E R L E ▪ T H E M ▪ ▪ E N Y A
```

10

```
P S S T ▪ S P A R ▪ A M E S
R E P O ▪ S H O R E ▪ L E S S
E V A N ▪ M I S S P R I N T S
F E R ▪ D I E S ▪ S A N T A
A R K W E L D E R ▪ M E H T A
B A L I N E ▪ A L P ▪ O E D
▪ L E T S ▪ S A S E ▪ A L S O
▪ ▪ T E N N S P E E D ▪ ▪
S P R Y ▪ C O P Y ▪ R A I N
O R O ▪ O O O ▪ S U N D A E
C O M I C ▪ P E N N P O I N T
▪ B A N T U ▪ W A I T ▪ A K U
C O N N A R T I S T ▪ A M I D
O N C E ▪ G E N T S ▪ P I N E
D O E R ▪ E D G Y ▪ E N G S
```

11

```
S P I T   M A B E L   D I A L
T O D O   O P E R A   I D L E
D O O M   C H E A T   M E A T
  F L A S H I N T H E P A N
    H E A D     E L L
P L E A T   S U B   F E T C H
A I R W A Y   T A P     S O U
S N A K E I N T H E G R A S S
S E T   P E E   A L E R T S
E R O D E   O R B   A S S A Y
    E T S     A C R E
  S T I C K I N T H E M U D
C H I C   A B A T E   B R I M
S I D E   T I M E S   L A V A
A V E R   E D E N S   E L A N
```

12

```
L A P P   W E D G E   A S A P
A L L Y   A X I A L   R A C E
H O U R G L A S S F I G U R E
R E S E A R C H   R Y D E R
      R U T   B A I L
C A L A I S   F A L S E T T O
A W A C S   K A T E   R E P
W A T C H O N T H E R H I N E
E K E   L E E S   E A T O N
D E R A N G E D   A N G E R S
    F O A L   A N D
M E N L O   A S T E R O I D
C L O C K W O R K O R A N G E
A L I I   A L I E N   S T O P
N E R O   R E A D Y   P O R T
```

13

```
T I L E   B E L L   A N G R Y
A V E R   O D I E   M E L E E
M I N I   G N A W   I D E A L
P E A C E G A R D E N   E L L
A S S A I L     R O T C
      G E R M A N   O L G A
R A J A H   E A S E   Q U I D
A P O R T   L I S   B U B B A
K A Y E   H A Z E   Y E S E S
E L B A   E X E T E R
    U S E R   L O C A L E
B I Z   L O V E H A N D L E S
O O Z E D   A R A T   R I M S
S T E V E   S I T E   O B O E
C A R E R   T E E D   M I N N
```

14

```
O L D S   C O L I C   T A C K
D A R T   A F A C T   E L H I
D R E S S B L U E S   R I A L
S K A   L I A R   S M E L T
  M O U N T A I N P I N K S
C H I N E S E   S E A N
P O E T S   A I R R I F L E
A S S   A L L T O   L E N
S T T H O M A S   F R I T Z
  O M E N   A G R E E T O
C O L L A R D G R E E N S
O S I E R   A C R E   A A A
S H O O   H A S H B R O W N S
M E N U   E L S I E   D A T E
O A S T   P A Y E R   E Y E S
```

15

```
A R T S   W I P E   C A B I N
N E A T   E R I N   A G A T E
D E C R E A S E D   Y E A S T
A L I E N S   D U P E
  S T A V E S   P A N A M A
    M O L A R   I N S A N E
F U S S Y   D E P R E S S E D
A S P   C A P E S   E N G
D E L I G H T E D   D I R T Y
E R A S E R   G R O O M
  S T A T I C   O R N A T E
    A S I F   A N G O L A
E N D O W   D E C L A I M E D
T I A R A   E T A L   N E N E
A B B E Y   R E L Y   E S A S
```

16

GASP ELVIS PECK
ITTO COINS EVAN
JOINTOWNER NERO
OMEGA MED SHREW
ESS LEADINTO
CORN BEELINE
OCTANE BLENDSIN
TORN CREED EINE
TOOOFTEN LORNES
OLDPROS HESS
EARLIEST AGE
SCANT ALA EBBED
PACE STIRFRYING
OVER TEASE EDIE
TEDS ADDER SEES

17

PLUMB CLV BLAH
RESAY LAI BOISE
IMADEHIMANOFFER
AMI AMP INFEAR
MARLONBRANDO
ARK ETE YES
ALENE DYER CORP
WELCOME ASTORIA
RAKE ABAT AMENS
YRS BUD ARE
THEGODFATHER
SPIRAL RIA ODE
HECOULDNTREFUSE
ALEUT JET PANES
WEST SRO ADDLE

18

REST TECHS CHAD
EVER AFLAT HOBO
VANITYFAIR ROBS
UNSOILED NOFEE
ESE TOT CAIN
BUREAUCHIEFS
APERS GRE CLOP
LENA MORES LALA
EATS AGE MENDS
CROSSDRESSER
BIDE PAD JIF
GETAT MANITOBA
ALAN HAIRYCHEST
BIND ROMEO ALES
SAGS SLEDS ISNO

19

SERFS LIRA SCAM
TRAIT ODOR POLE
RACER TEAT ALIT
ASKFORHERHAND
WES KEA ARC WPA
HEARTTOHEART
ARTE CIO ENTER
ROWS TOWIT SEEA
MOOSE ENE URNS
ONBENDEDKNEE
REY DAY STL GAB
FOOTEDTHEBILL
COOL ELIA CALLA
THUD REMI TIDES
SORE STEN SLANT

20

SLAT CRAM DOONE
HAIR RIGA UPTON
USDA ITER RATIO
THELASTEMPEROR
ALTE OAST
ARG FORESTS KIM
LEROI AEC NANA
ALIFEFORTHECZAR
REST RUT LOOPY
MET BETHUNE OTS
TEAR RONS
CHICKENALAKING
PLINK AONE ONIN
CADGE CPUS ATTA
SWEET HESS LOST

21

BODE · SPEND · SECT
RHOS · ERROR · ALAS
AINT · PETROUCHKA
COQUETTE · INKIER
· UAR · · DEF ·
EMIRATES · SAUNAS
WAXY · ALTO · SLUMP
ENO · GISELLE · TAO
RETRO · ARIA · ACID
STEELY · NOCTURNE
· ODE · · ARA ·
IBERIA · BARBECUE
CINDERELLA · OKLA
EDGE · NEALS · LENS
TERR · SLUSH · ERAT

22

SUM · MOAT · STRAW
ERI · UNBAR · QUICK
DAM · SEATO · URGES
UNOWHATIMEAN
CUSHY · EBB · IMA
ESAI · RESOW · BRAG
· PEELE · HORACE
· DOSOFMEDICINE
JEJUNE · DITTO
REAP · RHYME · CRIB
SRI · TEA · SHANE
· TRESELEMENTS
ARMEY · TRUCE · CUT
LIARS · ERROL · ONE
TAINT · SENT · RED

23

DECAF · ADLIB · LUV
ELISE · DIANA · ASA
LOOSELIPPED · MET
· LAOS · LEEDS
FASTENS · CRUMB
ENTIRE · ELECTRON
LYRES · PLUNK · ACE
LOOS · FILED · MITT
ANN · PINES · SENAT
SEGMENTS · SERENE
· ATSEA · SECEDED
VERSE · PART ·
CAM · TIGHTFISTED
RTE · ATREE · ORONO
SAD · STOWS · NONET

24

GAPE · MEAL · SMITH
ORAN · ELMO · HANOI
WILD · LIFTTICKET
NEMESIS · TYNE
· LSATS · ROPE · PAM
· PRESTO · ERMINE
TAR · RABBLE · INGA
AVIAN · ALE · TACIT
SONY · EROICA · HEY
SIGNAL · WARMUP
EDS · TIRE · APPLE
· SHOO · SNARERS
POCKETBOOK · IAMA
JAPAN · OBOE · STAG
STATS · TEND · ESSE

25

PITH · MORAL · IPSO
SOHO · CRATE · FUNK
SWINGINGONASTAR
TASKS · AGLOW · OPA
· YEA · MEL · EON
FEED · BEDS · START
ALA · EENY · KOSHER
GER · NET · DIM · AMI
INSIST · CODE · PUP
NIKON · COBS · APSE
· INA · AMA · PLY
ASS · REMIT · REFER
ITSALLINTHEGAME
NOEL · ANGLE · ACME
TASS · NOSES · REAL

26

A	H	A	B	■	L	I	M	P	■	P	L	A	N	B
N	O	L	A	■	A	R	I	A	■	O	A	S	E	S
K	N	O	B	■	P	O	N	T	■	S	C	H	W	A
A	G	E	O	F	A	N	X	I	E	T	Y	■	■	■
■	■	■	O	R	L	Y	■	O	N	A	■	J	O	G
■	V	E	N	O	M	■	■	I	G	N	O	R	E	■
M	I	A	■	M	A	U	V	E	D	E	C	A	D	E
A	R	T	S	■	■	G	E	T	■	O	N	E	S	■
G	A	S	L	I	G	H	T	E	R	A	■	N	A	E
I	G	U	A	N	A	■	■	E	Q	U	A	L	■	■
C	O	P	■	T	N	T	■	S	T	U	N	■	■	■
■	■	M	E	G	E	N	E	R	A	T	I	O	N	■
K	A	Z	A	N	■	N	O	T	A	■	O	S	L	O
A	D	A	M	S	■	E	P	I	C	■	L	E	G	O
T	E	P	E	E	■	T	E	N	T	■	D	E	A	R

27

H	O	L	E	■	S	T	I	L	L	■	I	S	M	S
A	P	A	R	■	A	E	R	I	E	■	D	Y	A	N
L	E	V	I	■	L	A	K	E	G	E	O	R	G	E
F	R	A	N	C	I	S	■	G	A	D	■	U	N	E
■	■	■	G	O	V	■	F	E	L	D	S	P	A	R
P	A	N	O	R	A	M	A	■	L	A	T	■	■	■
A	D	O	B	E	■	A	B	L	Y	■	P	A	I	N
P	O	O	R	S	■	I	F	A	■	F	A	U	R	E
A	S	K	A	■	K	N	O	W	■	L	U	N	A	R
■	■	■	G	H	I	■	U	N	B	O	L	T	E	D
B	A	C	H	E	L	O	R	■	U	R	I	■	■	■
A	L	L	■	A	L	F	■	O	N	A	G	E	R	S
S	A	I	N	T	J	O	H	N	S	■	I	R	A	N
A	M	M	O	■	O	N	I	C	E	■	R	I	T	A
L	O	B	S	■	Y	E	M	E	N	■	L	E	A	P

28

L	I	S	P	S	■	S	P	E	C	■	D	I	V	A
E	C	L	A	T	■	T	I	L	E	■	O	B	I	S
S	O	U	P	A	N	D	S	A	N	D	W	I	C	H
E	N	G	A	G	E	■	A	T	T	E	N	D	E	E
■	■	■	L	E	A	R	■	E	R	A	S	■	■	■
C	B	S	■	S	T	E	M	■	I	N	T	A	K	E
O	U	T	S	■	E	E	O	C	■	N	A	M	E	D
M	E	A	T	A	N	D	P	O	T	A	T	O	E	S
E	N	D	E	R	■	S	E	C	S	■	E	R	L	E
T	O	T	E	M	S	■	D	O	E	S	■	Y	S	L
■	■	■	L	A	L	A	■	A	T	U	B	■	■	■
R	E	S	I	D	I	N	G	■	S	C	A	L	P	S
C	A	K	E	A	N	D	I	C	E	C	R	E	A	M
A	S	I	S	■	G	U	L	P	■	O	R	A	T	E
S	E	N	T	■	S	P	A	R	■	R	E	N	E	W

29

C	A	P	R	I	■	E	G	G	■	P	A	T	T	Y
U	N	I	O	N	■	S	I	R	■	O	M	A	H	A
S	T	E	M	S	■	A	L	I	■	L	A	X	E	R
P	E	R	P	E	T	U	A	L	M	O	T	I	O	N
■	■	■	S	C	I	■	S	L	I	P	■	■	■	■
I	S	H	■	T	A	X	■	E	X	O	T	I	C	A
N	C	A	A	■	R	I	G	■	■	N	O	N	O	S
F	O	U	N	T	A	I	N	O	F	Y	O	U	T	H
R	U	N	T	O	■	U	N	E	■	K	I	T	E	■
A	T	T	I	M	E	S	■	A	L	F	■	T	A	N
■	■	■	O	P	I	E	■	O	U	R	■	■	■	■
P	R	O	G	R	A	M	M	I	N	G	A	V	C	R
E	E	L	E	R	■	I	A	N	■	E	V	E	R	Y
A	M	I	N	O	■	L	I	T	■	E	E	R	I	E
S	I	N	E	W	■	E	L	O	■	S	L	O	B	S

30

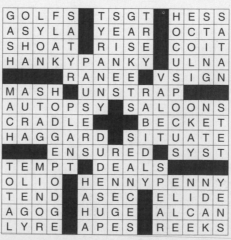

G	O	L	F	S	■	T	S	G	T	■	H	E	S	S
A	S	Y	L	A	■	Y	E	A	R	■	O	C	T	A
S	H	O	A	T	■	R	I	S	E	■	C	O	I	T
H	A	N	K	Y	P	A	N	K	Y	■	U	L	N	A
■	■	■	R	A	N	E	E	■	V	S	I	G	N	■
M	A	S	H	■	U	N	S	T	R	A	P	■	■	■
A	U	T	O	P	S	Y	■	S	A	L	O	O	N	S
C	R	A	D	L	E	■	■	B	E	C	K	E	T	■
H	A	G	G	A	R	D	■	S	I	T	U	A	T	E
■	■	■	E	N	S	U	R	E	D	■	S	Y	S	T
T	E	M	P	T	■	D	E	A	L	S	■	■	■	■
O	L	I	O	■	H	E	N	N	Y	P	E	N	N	Y
T	E	N	D	■	A	S	E	C	■	E	L	I	D	E
A	G	O	G	■	H	U	G	E	■	A	L	C	A	N
L	Y	R	E	■	A	P	E	S	■	R	E	E	K	S

31

```
S L O T   P R A M   S C A L P
L I V E   R A R E   T A B O O
A M E N   A S I S   O B E S E
V E R O N I C A S C L O S E T
    R O S A     L I T
N A W   R E L A T E D   L A P
O P A R T   N R A   D E C A
M A R T H A S V I N E Y A R D
A C M E   L A I   N E V E R
D E S   C O L L A R D   E S E
    R A F     R O O T
C H R I S T I N A S W O R L D
R O A S T   D E B T   T O U R
A N G E L   E R I E   A L V A
G E E S E   S O A R   L E S T
```

32

```
S H A W   S C A T S   V A S T
H O L O   C O R O T   O N T O
O R E M   A D I M E   O D E S
O N E A R M E D B A N D I T S
      N A P     D O O
L I C I T   S A S   T O S C A
I R R S   A U D I T S   O R B
T W O H A N D E D V O L L E Y
R I O   S T A L L S   O T T S
E N N U I   N E E   I V I E S
      S D S     N N E
T H R E E L E G G E D R A C E
H O E S   O V A L S   B U L L
U R D U   B E G O T   O R E L
G A S P   S L A B S   Y A M S
```

33

```
A S T A   P E P S   C L I P
P L O P   A I L E Y   A O N E
S U N R I S E S E R E N A D E
E G O   A T P A R   V I N Y L
    A G R A     D A N
T H E N O O N D A Y D E V I L
H E W N   W H E E   I M A
I L I E   B R A S S   P R A Y
R I N   L A I R   E G G O
D O G D A Y A F T E R N O O N
    E L S   H I E D
S A M B A   B R I G S   B I C
T H E T W I L I G H T Z O N E
I M S O   R I G H T   O A F S
R E A R   S P A S   T R O T
```

34

```
A B B O T   R A J A S   G E L
C O R N S   E R A T O   A N O
Q U I C K D R A W M C G R A W
U R G E   R U B S   C I R C E
I S H   H E N S   H E L O T S
T E T R A   M A R   T E T
    O R A C L E S   B E D
    S W I F T Y L A Z A R
    B U S   O R E S T E S
G A R   A R S   R E E L S
A D M I R E   F A R O   D E O
F L I N G   E L L E   F I N N
F A S T E D D I E F E L S O N
E N E   N I G E R   M O O R E
R D S   T R Y S T   T E N E T
```

35

```
M A M A S   F R O M   F A M E
A G I L E   R A R A   O L E G
R O N E E   E G A N   U P T O
K N U C K L E U N D E R
S Y S   E A R   G Y N   C A B
    A R N E S S   A T R I A
A C E D   D I E   S C R O L L
T H R O W I N T H E T O W E L
T I A R A S   T E A   O D D S
A N S E L   R O L L U P
R A E   L I E   P A N   A L L
    E A T H U M B L E P I E
B R E D   S E R A   E X A C T
R A N G   M E A T   S P R I G
A H O Y   E L L E   S O T T O
```

36

```
A L P S . W E E D . M E L E E
N E A T . E L M O . O L A N D
I T T O . R I O T . D A Z E D
T H E G R E A T E N E M Y . .
A E R I E . . E L A L . S P F
. . E X A M . L E I S U R E .
D A S . . H I P . N O S E D .
O F C L E A R L A N G U A G E
B L O O M . . Y O U . . N O X
B A R B A R Y . K N O T . . .
S T P . C O E D . W E L S H .
. . I S I N S I N C E R I T Y
A L O H A . M A I L . C L A P
T E N E T . A N N A . E L L E
M A S S E . N E E D . L E E R
```

37

```
R U S H . B R I M . C L E F T
A T T A . E A S E . R A T E R
P A I N . A S I S . I T A L Y
T H R O U G H T H E M I L L .
. . I S L E . . D E N . . . .
F D A . H E R A L D S . A T T
L U N G E . . D O I . A C R E
U N D E R T H E W E A T H E R
T E E M . H O P . T E E N S .
E S S . C O N T E S T . D D E
. . F O R . T H I S . . . . .
. A R O U N D T H E C L O C K
C L E A R . E R I E . I R A N
B O I L S . P I C T . C A R E
S E N S E . T O S S . E L S E
```

38

```
E N C L A V E . U G H . A R E
F R A I L E R . B R O . R O N
T A L K E D A B O U T . C U D
. D E C I . O L E . C A T O .
G I R L S C O U T L E A D E R
A M O Y . M T S . C B E R S .
P A N . N O N O . G R O S S E
. H I D I N G O U T . . . . .
O C T A N E . N U T S . S A P
B R E S T . T I S . S E M I .
S O U T H V I E T N A M E S E
C U T E . O E R . A L I T . .
E T O . W I D E M O U T H E D
N O N . I C Y . I M M E R S E
E N S . G E E . T I S S U E S
```

39

```
M U F T I . P E A K . D E J A
A G R I N . O S S A . E V E S
T H E S H I P P I N G N E W S
T S E . A S P . A G A I N S T
. F O R M E D . A P E . . . .
S L O A N . D E A R . D U A L
C A R T E L . F R O M . N N E
A P A S S A G E T O I N D I A
R E L . S T A N . S L E E T S
E L L A . E L S E . K A R A T
. T E C . E X I S T S . . . .
S T E T S O N . P A H . T B S
T H R E E M E N I N A B O A T
E A R S . E V E R . K O O K Y
M I S T . R A T E . E N D U E
```

40

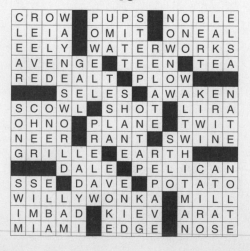

```
C R O W . P U P S . N O B L E
L E I A . O M I T . O N E A L
E E L Y . W A T E R W O R K S
A V E N G E . T E E N . T E A
R E D E A L T . P L O W . . .
. . S E L E S . A W A K E N .
S C O W L . S H O T . L I R A
O H N O . P L A N E . T W I T
N E E R . R A N T . S W I N E
G R I L L E . E A R T H . . .
. . D A L E . P E L I C A N .
S S E . D A V E . P O T A T O
W I L L Y W O N K A . M I L L
I M B A D . K I E V . A R A T
M I A M I . E D G E . N O S E
```

41

K	H	A	N		M	O	M	A		P	A	C	E	R
N	O	D	E		E	R	I	C		A	D	A	L	E
O	L	D	A	S	M	E	T	H	U	S	E	L	A	H
X	E	S		C	O	M	E	O	N		N	A	P	E
		F	R	I		S	O	F	T		I	S	M	
O	C	U	L	A	R	S			E	R	A	S	E	
N	E	W	A	M	S	T	E	R	D	A	M			
T	E	E	M			A	G	O		Y	E	A	R	
	B	O	R	R	O	W	E	D	T	I	M	E		
	G	R	E	T	A		S	N	E	A	K	I	N	
I	R	E		O	K	L	A		C	N	N			
N	I	P	S		E	L	L	I	O	T		Z	I	G
B	L	U	E	G	R	A	S	S	R	E	G	I	O	N
A	L	T	A	R		M	O	L	E		A	N	N	A
D	E	E	R	E		A	P	E	S		S	C	A	T

42

T	O	G	O		A	B	R	A	M		P	A	R	K
O	V	E	R		F	R	O	D	O		O	K	A	Y
G	A	R	B	A	G	E	P	A	I	L	K	I	D	S
A	L	M	I	G	H	T	Y		E	E	R	I	E	
	T	H	A	T		D	E	A	D	A	I	R		
K	O	R	E	A	N		V	O	D	K	A			
O	P	E	D	S		M	I	N	I		T	U	C	K
F	E	D		T	R	A	S	H	T	V		T	O	A
C	R	O	P		O	L	E	O		I	F	N	O	T
	R	A	I	L	S		S	O	R	E	L	Y		
D	E	M	I	L	L	E		G	A	L	A			
O	N	I	C	E		O	I	L	I	N	E	S	S	
J	U	N	K	F	O	O	D	J	U	N	K	I	E	S
O	R	E	L		E	L	I	O	T		O	N	E	R
S	E	R	E		R	E	N	E	E		Z	E	D	S

43

B	E	E	T		S	C	A	M		B	O	A	S	T
A	C	R	E		H	O	S	E		E	A	G	E	R
C	R	O	C		R	O	A	D		A	R	E	N	A
H	U	S	H	P	U	P	P	I	E	S		S	T	Y
		A	B	U		A	N	T	S					
C	A	B	I	N		P	I	T	T		E	L	A	L
A	P	O	G	E	E		N	E	A		R	I	L	E
S	O	U	N	D	S	O	F	S	I	L	E	N	C	E
A	R	L	O		C	U	E		L	I	N	E	A	R
S	T	E	R		O	T	R	O		B	E	N	N	Y
		E	A	R	S		B	O	Y					
E	G	G		S	T	I	L	L	W	A	T	E	R	S
D	O	N	U	T		D	O	I	N		H	A	U	L
E	R	A	S	E		E	D	G	E		I	S	L	E
N	E	W	E	R		R	E	E	D		S	T	E	W

44

E	A	S	T		M	A	K	E	S		A	S	A	P
N	E	A	R		E	L	I	T	E		M	Y	N	A
I	N	F	O		A	L	E	U	T		O	M	A	N
G	E	E	N	A	D	A	V	I	S	C	U	P		
M	A	T		L	E	N			P	R	O	B	E	
A	S	Y	E	T		C	E	L	L		S	U	M	
	E	A	G	E	R	L	Y		A	I	R	S		
	P	E	R	R	Y	M	A	S	O	N	J	A	R	
F	O	X	Y		R	U	M	A	N	I	A			
A	S	H		M	O	S	S		E	X	U	L	T	
B	E	I	G	E		S	E	C		S	O	I		
	B	I	L	L	Y	R	O	S	E	B	O	W	L	
H	A	I	G		I	V	A	N	S		O	P	E	D
A	L	T	O		S	E	P	I	A		N	E	N	E
G	I	S	T		A	S	S	A	Y		A	N	D	S

45

A	L	I	B	I		L	A	M	B		Q	A	I	D
M	I	L	A	N		O	N	E	A		U	N	T	O
A	M	E	N	S		B	O	A	Z		E	K	E	S
T	A	X	A	T	I	O	N	L	A	W	S	A	R	E
			L	E	G		A	C	T					
A	M	A		A	L	A		A	R	T		A	F	L
B	A	S	E	D	U	P	O	N	S	U	P	P	L	Y
E	N	I	D		I	W	O		I	R	A	S		
A	N	D	D	E	M	A	N	D	T	H	E	I	R	S
M	A	E		V	A	N		E	R	A		L	E	A
	B	A	N			E	N	E						
D	E	M	A	N	D	S	W	E	S	U	P	P	L	Y
A	R	A	B		A	L	A	N		K	O	R	E	A
R	I	C	E		T	O	D	D		A	X	I	O	M
K	E	E	L		E	W	E	S		H	Y	M	N	S

46

```
B A N G ▪ A M A S S ▪ E A S T
A G E E ▪ M A C R O ▪ I N C A
B U L L D U R H A M ▪ G N A T
E E L ▪ A L I E ▪ E T H A N E
▪ ▪ ▪ D I E S ▪ S T A T ▪ ▪ ▪
A G H A S T ▪ S W I M M E R S
F O A M Y ▪ T H E M ▪ E V E L
T O R N ▪ T R A D E ▪ N A N A
E S P Y ▪ A O N E ▪ T O D A Y
R E S A M P L E ▪ G R U E L S
▪ ▪ N O E L ▪ P O E T ▪ ▪ ▪
S N A K E S ▪ M I C A ▪ O L E
P O L E ▪ T H E N A T U R A L
A L O E ▪ R I S E R ▪ R E D S
N O U S ▪ Y E A S T ▪ N O D E
```

47

```
A M O S ▪ C A R A T ▪ A M A S
B A B E ▪ A M A N A ▪ M O L T
B R O A D W A Y D I S P L A Y
A X E ▪ E D I E ▪ ▪ H E L I X
▪ ▪ ▪ E L O N ▪ O M A R ▪ ▪ ▪
M A H L E R ▪ A C A D E M I C
A B E E T ▪ G L E N ▪ ▪ E L I
S U R V E I L L A N C E A I D
U S O ▪ ▪ M I E N ▪ H A L V E
R E N E G A D E ▪ G A S S E R
▪ ▪ ▪ V O T E ▪ D O I T ▪ ▪ ▪
T H R O B ▪ C E L S ▪ J O E
B O O K I E S O F F E R I N G
A B B E ▪ C A N O E ▪ I N C A
R O B S ▪ O T T E R ▪ O X E N
```

48

```
M I A T A ▪ E R I N ▪ D E P P
A N G E L ▪ M E N O ▪ E L I A
P R I N C E O F T H E C I T Y
S E N ▪ I N T R O ▪ D R E S S
▪ ▪ ▪ O N C E A ▪ A M E ▪ ▪ ▪
T H E F A E R I E Q U E E N E
E A S T ▪ ▪ N O U N ▪ L O Y
M R S ▪ A L E ▪ S A D ▪ E L I
P E A ▪ G O G O ▪ ▪ O M A N
I D Y L L S O F T H E K I N G
▪ ▪ E E E ▪ F E E L S ▪ ▪ ▪
S I L V A ▪ H E N R I ▪ S L Y
T H E E M P E R O R J O N E S
L A N E ▪ L E E R ▪ A R I S E
O D D S ▪ O L D S ▪ H Y P E R
```

49

```
S T E M ▪ C L O Y ▪ ▪ J A K E
L O D I ▪ R A V E S ▪ E M I T
E N G A G E M E N T S T O N E
W E E ▪ O P E N ▪ A P H I D S
▪ ▪ ▪ A L E ▪ ▪ B R E R ▪ ▪
E V E N A S A N A C C O U N T
M E L O N ▪ B A T H S ▪ T O Q
A R I D ▪ A N N O Y ▪ N I N A
I D O ▪ G L E N N ▪ S O L E D
L I T E R A R Y S O C I E T Y
▪ ▪ G E M S ▪ ▪ P H R ▪ ▪ ▪
S T E R E O ▪ S E E M ▪ A L F
L O V E R S I M B R O G L I O
U K E S ▪ A C U R A ▪ A P E X
M E S S ▪ E G O S ▪ B O N Y
```

50

```
T A B O O ▪ T A R T ▪ P O S H
S P E A R ▪ I D E A ▪ R U L E
P O L K A ▪ T A L L ▪ E G O S
▪ ▪ C R A Z Y E I G H T S
▪ S C A L E N E ▪ S O O T H E
F L A R E S ▪ H E W ▪ ▪ ▪
A U D I ▪ E M M A ▪ A L I S T
D R E S S T O T H E N I N E S
E S T E E ▪ B A A S ▪ B A N K
▪ ▪ ▪ I D S ▪ S T E N O S
A R C A N E ▪ S T E A L E R
P E R F E C T T E N S ▪ ▪
A L A R ▪ O R E L ▪ S A B E R
C A T O ▪ D I A L ▪ E B O N Y
E X E S ▪ E M M Y ▪ L E A S E
```

51

R	E	I	N		S	A	T	E			R	U	B	E
A	R	T	Y		E	X	I	L	E		A	L	A	N
B	A	S	E	B	A	L	L	I	N	F	I	E	L	D
E	T	A		A	L	E	E		C	O	S	E	T	S
		I	C	I			S	A	R	I				
P	E	R	S	O	N	W	H	O	S	U	N	H	I	P
A	L	I	E	N		H	A	R	E	M		A	R	A
T	I	G	E		G	I	S	T	S		E	G	A	N
H	H	H		L	O	T	T	O		A	C	U	T	E
O	U	T	S	I	D	E	O	F	A	W	H	E	E	L
		A	L	L	Y			L	O	O				
H	A	S	S	L	E		A	M	O	K		A	C	T
O	R	C	H	E	S	T	R	A	M	E	M	B	E	R
A	G	U	A		S	A	N	T	A		A	B	L	E
R	O	M	Y			J	E	E	R		W	A	L	K

52

R	A	G	E	D		R	A	I	D		V	I	A	L
A	R	O	M	A		O	N	C	E		I	N	R	E
F	I	L	I	B	U	S	T	E	R		O	T	I	S
T	S	A	R		R	Y	E			P	L	E	A	S
S	E	N	S	E	S			O	S	C	A	R		
				L	A	C	K	L	U	S	T	E	R	
A	C	R	E	S		A	I	D	E		I	S	I	S
F	L	E	X		A	C	T	E	D		O	T	T	O
T	O	N	I		R	T	E	S		A	N	S	E	L
	P	A	S	S	M	U	S	T	E	R				
		S	T	A	Y	S			Y	I	E	L	D	S
F	A	C	E	D			P	O	E		B	A	R	E
A	M	E	N		C	R	O	P	D	U	S	T	E	R
Z	I	N	C		H	E	R	E		R	E	H	A	B
E	S	T	E		E	D	E	N		E	N	E	R	O

53

S	E	W	E	D		M	O	S	H	E		T	I	P
E	L	A	T	E		O	O	H	E	D		A	L	I
C	H	I	C	K	E	N	F	E	E	D		P	I	A
T	I	T	H	E	S		E	L	Y	S	I	A	N	
			S	C	R	A	P	E		U	N	D	O	
S	L	O	W		R	U	M		R	O	K			
K	I	W	I		O	M	E	N		R	A	M	B	O
Y	E	L	L	O	W	B	R	I	C	K	R	O	A	D
S	U	S	H	I		A	C	L	U		N	O	L	O
	E	L	I		E	E	R		O	D	E	R		
B	A	W	L		N	E	S	S	I	E				
A	N	I	M	A	L	S		E	X	H	U	M	E	
L	A	T		S	I	S	S	Y	S	P	A	C	E	K
S	I	C		S	N	E	E	R		E	L	L	I	E
A	S	H		T	E	N	T	S		L	E	A	N	S

54

B	R	I	D	A	L		A	R	M	O	I	R	E	
A	E	R	A	T	E		C	H	E	S	T	E	R	
A	M	A	Z	O	N		S	E	T	H	O	M	A	S
			E	M	I	T		N	E	A		A	S	P
A	C	H		N	O	S	I	R		B	I	E	R	
R	H	O	D	A		U	S	S		W	E	N	D	Y
G	E	O	R	G	E	R	S	H	W	I	N			
O	R	D	A	I	N			O	L	D	I	E	S	
			P	L	A	C	I	D	O	M	I	N	G	O
O	H	G	E	E		A	D	O		A	X	I	O	M
L	E	A	D		S	T	A	F	F			T	S	E
E	L	I		S	A	C		F	A	T	E			
G	E	N	E	W	M	A	N		R	I	D	G	E	D
	N	O	T	A	B	L	E		E	L	N	I	N	O
A	N	O	M	A	L	Y		S	T	A	N	D	S	

55

W	A	N	E	D		C	R	A	N	K		B	A	T
E	M	I	L	E		A	A	R	O	N		A	G	E
B	A	L	L	S	O	F	F	I	R	E		R	A	N
		S	U	E	T			E	E	R	I	E		
P	O	W	D	E	R	S		A	P	P	O	I	N	T
O	T	H	E	R	S		S	L	O	A	N	E		
S	T	I	N	T		B	U	I	L	D		R	H	O
S	E	T	S		M	I	D	G	E		W	R	E	N
E	R	E		S	E	D	A	N		M	I	E	N	S
		S	A	T	E	E	N		S	E	V	E	R	E
T	S	H	I	R	T	S		B	E	N	E	F	I	T
O	H	A	R	E			B	O	L	A				
G	A	R		W	A	L	L	O	F	C	H	I	N	A
A	R	K		E	L	I	O	T		E	A	R	E	D
S	I	S		D	E	B	B	Y		S	P	E	E	D

56

```
M A P ■ A L D A ■ U P S H O T
O P E N D O O R ■ S L U I C E
M E T E O R I C ■ S E E T H E
■ R O B I N H O O D S M E N ■
C A I N E ■ ■ A L G ■ E R S ■
O R D ■ G U A R D E D ■ ■ ■
B R I M ■ I N C ■ I S A A C S
R O S A ■ R O U G E ■ I S L A
A W H I R L ■ T A R ■ S P I N
■ M A S T E R S ■ E M T ■ ■
E P A ■ I C H ■ ■ K O R E A ■
D A R T M O U T H F A N S ■
I N L I E U ■ W A R P A I N T
N E E D N T ■ O N E O N O N E
A S S E T S ■ S K E W ■ N E D
```

57

```
W R A P S ■ F L A T ■ S ⬦ I T
H O R A E ■ S U R E ■ S C A R
O U I J A ■ ⬦ T E N ■ R O M E
A T L A S T ■ E A T S ■ A B E
■ ■ M O E T ■ S H O R T S ⬦
C I L A N T R O ■ S A Y ■ ■
L A P ⬦ ■ R O N A ■ R E C A P
E G G ■ A U ⬦ S Y ■ A H A
F O A M Y ■ T O N E ■ ⬦ P E R
■ ■ B A R ■ F E A R S O M E
⬦ D R A W E R ■ R H E E ■ ■
S A O ■ N C A A ■ S I C K E N
I Z O D ■ T I P ⬦ ■ G R I P E
D E F T ■ O T I S ■ N E W E R
E S ⬦ S ■ S T A Y ■ S T I E D
```

58

```
I T S ■ S T O N E ■ O P E R A
N A T ■ P O D I A ■ S I X E S
S P A R E R I B S ■ U N C A P
E E R I E ■ E S T A ■ P E P S
T R E N D S ■ E R R O R ■ ■
■ G U T T E R S N I P E ■ ■
Y E A ■ P A I L ■ A N T I C
A R I A ■ G N O M E ■ T E R N
K A R L S ■ P A R S ■ D E N
■ S P L I T S E C O N D ■ ■
■ L E T U P ■ S O U R C E
S L A Y ■ T A U T ■ O D O R S
C A N O E ■ S T R I K E O U T
O L E O S ■ M A U V E ■ S S E
W A S P S ■ S H E E R ■ T H E
```

59

```
M U T E ■ M O O R ■ S P O O R
A P E X ■ E Z R A ■ C A L V E
E T N A ■ O M A N ■ A D D E D
N A N C Y W A L K E R ■ G R R
A K I T A ■ ■ L A S A L L E
D E S ■ R E A D E R ■ L O I S
■ ■ C R O N E ■ A I R E S
■ L E O N T R O T S K Y ■
S Q U A W ■ A W A K E ■ ■
C U T S ■ E A T E R Y ■ A S S
R E H E A R D ■ ■ O U N C E
E E E ■ D A M O N R U N Y O N
E N R O L ■ I D E A ■ M O O S
D I A N E ■ R O A M ■ A N T E
S E N O R ■ E R R S ■ N E S S
```

60

```
F A R O ■ S G T S ■ B R E A D
A M E X ■ T A I L ■ R E A V E
L I M E ■ I N R E ■ A P R E S
L E O N A R D O D A V I N C I
■ ■ H U H ■ ■ B A N ■ ■
L U I G I P I R A N D E L L O
A L L O T ■ O L E O ■ A I T
U C L A ■ C O M E R ■ W H E T
R E A ■ G L U E ■ M E T O O
A R T U R O T O S C A N I N I
■ ■ P E W ■ A L I ■ ■
V I N C E N Z O B E L L I N I
A D E A L ■ E L I A ■ I C E D
M E E S E ■ R A N T ■ M A X I
P A R T Y ■ O N E S ■ O N T O
```

61

```
A N S   Q U I P   C H I L D
T O U T   U L N A   R O D E O
O V E R C O M E S   A T L A S
M O Z A R T   S T A Y H E R E
    D A I S   A L O E
F R E E Z E U P   E L A P S E
E E L   E N D U P   A D L I B
A L E C   T A R O S   S A N S
R I G O R   N I K E S   T E E
S T Y L E S   M E L T D O W N
    D E K E   S T E R
G R A F F I T I   Z E A L O T
R E L E E   U N D E R G O E S
I N F E R   D O U R   S O D A
M O A T S   E N O S   S S R
```

62

```
T O R A H   D A U B   A B B A
A L O N E   A L P O   G R A M
T E N O R   K I S S   R A G A
    D E N O F T H I E V E S
T I D E W A T E R   D E A L S
E A U   I M A   E L S
A M B I T   B A A   U S A
    B A T H R O O M H U M O R
S I S   A I D   N A B O B
      P T L   L E S   E S E
S U G A R   S P A T T E R E D
C L O S E T E A T E R S
O T O S   R E N E   U T T E R
T R E E   I D E S   N E W S Y
S A Y S   P S S T   G R A C E
```

63

```
R E A C T   M E A N S   T A R
E N S U E   A A R O N   O N E
C O U P D E G R A C E   U S A
    O D E O N   T E S T E D
H U F F I N G   L U R I D L Y
U N I T E S   S E R E N E
L I N E S   G L A N D   S A P
C O D A   L O U P E   C U R E
E N E   B O N E S   T O I L E
    S E I N E S   S O U T E R
S T I N K E R   P O S S E S S
T H E S I S   E R N S T
A R C   N O M D E G U E R R E
G E L   I M A G E   P A I N E
E W E   S E V E N   S U G A R
```

64

```
D A D   A L A S K A   A S T A
A V E   R A R I N G   S M O G
N I P   S I N G E R B O O N E
C A T F O R O N E   U F O
E T H A N   L B S   T I C
D E S I   D I D S O   O H N O
    R E E S E   N I V E N S
    P E A C H C E N T E R
C H A S T E   C L E A R
H A L T   I T A L Y   D O G S
E L I   A T A   E U B I E
    M A R   P O K E R B E T S
S T O C K O P T I O N   Y A T
A I N T   B A I R N S   E N E
W A Y S   I N S I S T   D O T
```

65

```
Z E D S   S T E T S   A W O L
E C R U   K O D A K   D O L E
S T O P P I N G B Y W O O D S
T O P E R   E L L I P S E
    R O T C   E A S T
B B L   T O R T   B E I G E S
L I E   O D E O N   O R N E
O N A S N O W Y E V E N I N G
O G R E   S E V E N   D U E
M O N A D S   D E L L   S I R
    M E A L   R O I L
  M A L A R I A   S A B R A
R O B E R T F R O S T P O E M
A R C S   R E N D S   A R A M
J E S S   E R O D E   Z E R O
```

66

```
FIRST  SIDON  XIS
EBOLI  WROTE  RON
NISAN  EARTO  ANA
DDAYKRATION  YIP
   ELATES   BOAS
DEGREES   THAR
ELMS   OFFLIMITS
ALA  BLUEICE  NIP
FANLETTER   EGGO
  SAND   MOONSET
ONES   CHARTA
ROM  AFRAMEIBEAM
TWA  GLAZE  OLIVE
HAI  EATEN  SENOR
OYL  DWELT  EDENS
```

67

```
AFAR  ARDOR  MATS
NORA  PIECE  AQUI
GROVERCLEVELAND
LASER  EVA  LIBEL
EYE  ABSENCE  ARE
    ASA    ONE
 JAMESBUCHANAN
COPS  TORRE  SPOT
ARP  PERSONA  TOO
MELLO  NAP  DRESS
PLEASE    AZORES
  JOHNKENNEDY
SPAT  DIVOT  EXEC
ARCS  ELITE  NEED
WOKE  DOLED  TSKS
```

68

```
ROME  QUADS  SCAM
ALEX  UNDID  PETE
MINI  ABACI  OLES
SOUTHFORK  COLAS
   AFL  ECONOMY
YEAST  TYRONE
ALLIES  EER  RADS
MALL  PRADO  INRI
SLAV  AER  TASTES
  ERRANT  MMIII
GNARLED  USO
LOEWS  JACKKNIFE
OLGA  TULSA  ADIN
VOIR  ASPOT  DOJO
ESSE  STONE  ALIS
```

69

```
ADMAN  BLAH  TRAM
MEATY  LALO  AUTO
IFYOUWANTTOKNOW
STOP  ASA  STEINS
    AXE  ETHANE
HOURLY  FLUE
ASSAM  SERF  SIZE
THEVALUEOFMONEY
SADE  OILY  ALIKE
    SONS  CNOTES
 CAWING  DAY
AIRILY  EAT  ALEX
TRYTOBORROWSOME
ACAT  ISNT  HEMIN
DENY  NASH  OCALA
```

70

```
MAZE  OFFS  STATS
AMES  RARE  TOLET
MISTERBIG  OPINE
ASTER  ISO  OBESE
   SNEAK  PLANER
SAG  INN  PAIN
EVENER  POLEAXES
PERU  OBOES  NILE
TREMBLED  IRANIS
  EELY  BEI  GAS
SPARES  BADGE
TAROT  OWN  ONSET
ASOUL  MAJORDOMO
ISONE  ANON  ELMO
DEMOS  NAST  DEAL
```

71

H A D J	W I N D	B R E E D
E L I A	I C E R	R A L L Y
M I S C	L I L Y T O M L I N
P I C K E D	L E O N	E S E
P E R E	R A Z Z
P A R A G O N S	D E S A D E
E T A L	S O L O	R A T O N
L A D A	E R E C T	Z O N E
F L I N G	M E T E	S L U R
S L I C E S	P A L O A L T O
E T A T	D E N G
A B A	A R I A	G E A R U P
G E N E W I L D E R	B O N E
U L T R A	E Z R A	O M I T
E L E G Y	S E A M	R A T E

72

L A P P S	L O A F	G A R P
I S L A M	E M M A	E L I A
V I O L A	R A I N	N E L L
A D O Z E N R E D R O S E S
M E R E	A A A
A S T I	A R D E N T	A N D
L L A N O	I N G E	L I U
B O X O F C H O C O L A T E S
A P E	F O O D	S P E C K
N E D	I N T E R N	P R E Y
E N D	O E I L
E N G A G E M E N T R I N G
X O U T	N E R D	A Q U A S
A N T I	S A M E	T U L L E
M O S T	E T A L	E E L E R

73

M A R C	W O R D	E S T E E
A S E A	A R I A	C H E A T
I T E M	F A C T	L A S S O
L I F E O F T H E P A R T Y
O S L O	R I P
C A T	T E R R I E R	A S H
A G A T E	E L L	U L N A
P I C K O F T H E L I T T E R
O L I O	A R A	R E A L M
N E T	T R I B U N E	R L S
S A G	S E N D
S A L T O F T H E E A R T H
C A R A T	R E E D	R A R E
O L I V E	E A R L	T I E R
S E D E R	E L S E	S L E D

74

C A R A	D E G S	S L I D E
A H E M	O G L E	T I M E R
D O L E	W A I T	I C I E R
G R I N A N D B A R E I T
E S E	C B S	E S T A T E
D E F A C E	R U B	B E D
C E A S E S	V A L E S
H O I S T T H E S A L E S
W A R D S	E A S E U P
O L D	O M B	C L O V E R
E L E C T S	T U T	E V E
R A Z E Y O U R S I T E S
C H I N A	A B L E	D O N E
H O N O R	M I S S	L E S T
E D G E S	S T A T	E R O S

75

D U Z	E R G	E K I S T I C
E D A	V E E	S A L E R N O
C A P	E V E	A M E R I N D
A L P I N E S K I I N G
F L A G	R E A	K E E L E R
E B B	R C A	I D A
M U S T Y	B O Y Z I I M E N
O R I N O C O	L E M M I N G
J A C O B R I I S	P A T S Y
O W E	I L S	M S G
S A M I A M	I F I	E A V E
S H I I T E M U S L I M
R E P A I N T	D O T	O R E
T R O I K A S	U S A	O A R
S N I D E L Y	P A H	F L Y